CELEBRATING LITERACY
IN THE RWENZORI REGION

CELEBRATING LITERACY IN THE RWENZORI REGION

(SECOND EDITION)

Lest We Forget: a Biographical Narrative of Uganda's Youngest Member of Parliament, 1980-1985

Amos Mubunga Kambere

Celebrating Literacy in the Rwenzori Region (Second Edition)
Lest We Forget: a Biographical Narrative of Uganda's Youngest Member of Parliament, 1980-1985
Copyright © 2020 by Amos Mubunga Kambere

Library of Congress Control Number: 2020903277
ISBN-13:   Paperback: 978-1-64749-060-7

Educational/Politics

All rights reserved. No part of this publication may be reproduced, distributed, or transmitted in any form or by any means, including photocopying, recording, or other electronic or mechanical methods, without the prior written permission of the publisher or author, except in the case of brief quotations embodied in critical reviews and certain other noncommercial uses permitted by copyright law.

Although every precaution has been taken to verify the accuracy of the information contained herein, the author and publisher assume no responsibility for any errors or omissions. No liability is assumed for damages that may result from the use of information contained within.

Printed in the United States of America

GoToPublish LLC
1-888-337-1724
www.gotopublish.com
info@gotopublish.com

Contents

Foreword ix
Dedication and Acknowledgement xi
Introduction xii
Chapter 1 1
Chapter 2 4
Chapter 3 13
Chapter 4 17
Chapter 5 24
Chapter 6 33
Chapter 7 43
Chapter 8 50
Chapter 9 59
- *The Gate way to Education – The third class train voyage*

Chapter 10 63
- *From the National Teachers University to National Assembly of Uganda [1978 -1984]*

Chapter 11 73
- *The 1980 election*

Chapter 12 86
- *Education: the Prerequisite for Development*

Chapter 13 97
- *Politics and the Church: Kasese was no exception*

Chapter 14 102
- *Rwenzururu: The final episode*

Chapter 15 110
- *The 1985 Coup D'état*

Chapter 16 117
- *From Prison to Praise*
- *Life in Luzira*

Chapter 17 128
- *The Ultimate Escape*

Chapter 18 134
- *From Freedom to Prison – Second Episode.*

Chapter 19 142
- *The undeniable God given "Ts"*

Chapter 20 149
- *Formation of Partnerships*
- *The Micro Finance success story:*

Chapter 21 155
- *OBUSINGA BWA RWENZURURU (RWENZURURU KINGDOM) AFTER RECOGNITION*
- *BACKGROUND OF THE RWENZURURU MOVEMENT*

Chapter 22 160
- *CONFLICT IN THE RWENZURURU UNITED KINGDOM*
- *THE CURRENT IMPASSE IN THE RWENZORI REGION*

Chapter 23 167
- *Fresh Issues of Conflict*
- *GENERAL OBSERVATIONS*

Chapter 24 172
- *Internal Conflict and Chaotic Executive Leadership*

Chapter 25 176
- *A Queen Mother Dies, and Chaos Erupts*

Chapter 26 180
- *The Journey to redemption*

Epilogue 182
- *The Unforgettable Myth Became REAL*

CELEBRATING LITERACY IN THE RWENZORI REGION
Lest we forget

A biographical narrative of Uganda's youngest Member of Parliament 1980-85
Amos Mubunga Kambere

Foreword

Lest we forget indeed! The immediate aftermath of the active militant Rwenzururu struggle saw a phenomenal awakening in development in the Rwenzori region as a whole. The most glaring example of such progress was in the field of education. Through collaborative effort on the part of the politicians, the technocrats and the entire population, a lot was achieved. In four short years, there were eight Government grant-aided secondary schools (in place of one), two partially grant-aided secondary schools and one private secondary school; two primary teacher training colleges and a technical school. One of the secondary schools was A-level status.

In this short narrative, the writer has labored to relate the process by which these achievements were made and enriched it by making it a personal autobiography. It becomes all the more important when it is borne in mind that he was the youngest member of the 3rd parliament of Uganda during this phenomenal period.

While it is not strictly a historical narrative, it certainly is historic. It at once brings into view the status of education in the region on the eve of Uganda's independence and explains that *status quo*. It is the work of a teacher-cum-politician and of necessity, it combines both. As a teacher, he orders his story while as a politician, he highlights selected aspects.

Whereas the geographical scope is the Rwenzori region, more attention is given to the writer's zone of jurisdiction, Kasese. But the reader should generalize for Bundibugyo, bearing in mind that the cause of the bitterness covered the whole region.

The stage is systematically set to prepare for both the development of the region and the autobiography. No development could have taken place when the local people were not in control of their own destiny. Nor could it take place when there was war going on. So peace had to be sought at first. This search for peace was ironically characterized by violence. The process brought on the scene two young men who tirelessly worked to bring about peace.

Unfortunately their continued development efforts were terminated by events at national level. It is this stage that the autobiography takes centre stage. The things that Amos personally suffered made him look at life differently. He received a baptism of fire through which he relocated both spiritually and physically. This relocation offered the necessary peace and facilitation to produce this work.

Celebrating Literacy in the Rwenzori region is an eye-opener to all the people in the region. With collaborative effort and stamina God will always bless our endeavors.

Enoch Sekalombi Muhindo

Dedication and Acknowledgement

This book is dedicated to my grand mother Georgina, my mother Julia, and my wife Edith who pray for my family unceasingly.

I would like to acknowledge and thank King Charles for providing me with accurate information regarding his father the late Isaya. I want to thank Jim Enoch Muhindo for being there during the hard times of formulating our developmental programs, Sande Nelson, Eva Bwambale, Dr.Syahuka-Muhindo Rev. Nelson Baliira, Dan Kashagama for encouraging me to write this book after listening to a short story about Kasese Elections; Penny Coates for igniting my passion to serve the immigrant community through the Make Children First initiative in Surrey, numerous volunteers who helped shape the work of developing partnerships; Nicole Mudri, Janice Hicks and Brandon Chenowas for venturing to stay in Rwentutu village developing literacy program for young kids, the teachers at Herbert Spencer Elementary school, Ms Tracy Fulton an Sharlene Briggs as well as all those I might have asked a few questions regarding the work of this book. You are all appreciated. Finally, to my father Fenehasi Mubunga who went with me on the gateway train to the city to seek the education that my district could not provide.

Introduction

This book is focused on the people of Kasese and Bundibugyo Districts, found on the foothills of the Mountains of the Moon. These people who cover the entire mountain range in both Uganda and the Democratic Republic of Congo, suffered greatly during the colonial period from the early 1890s to the early 1960s. In Uganda especially, this suffering was characterized by discrimination, segregation, marginalization and general neglect in all aspects of life. Education which was used as a vehicle of social change elsewhere in the country was deliberately denied.

On the eve of national independence in 1962 the people of the region demanded for self determination by getting separated from the Toro kingdom administration under which the British had colonized them. Unfortunately, the colonial government was too busy working out the modalities of ending their rule, to pay appropriate attention to this demand. This forced the people of the region into outright armed rebellion that lasted for twenty years.

In 1982 the leaders of the armed rebellion changed their method of struggle, ending twenty years of bitterness. The four short years that followed saw unprecedented development in many aspects of the social well being of the people in the region and most especially in the field of education.

The world is enormous, and everything we do to create a worldwide view broadens our horizons, and our choices for living and learning. Expanding our scope of thinking and learning makes life more fun and worth a living. This can only be achieved through education and, denying education to the people of the Ruwenzori was to limit their horizons and even their perception of themselves as human beings. This book will try to explain the circumstances that led to this plight.

The people on the slopes of Mt. Rwenzori [internationally known as the Mountains of the Moon], lived in their small world, narrow in scope and restricted in its consciousness, limited in its horizons, so that in effect, they created a little universe of their own. It was quite easy to live in a small confined, self-centered world. And, it was safe to exist this way before the intrusion of colonization from Europe. However, as soon as the rebellion opened their eyes the people became more aware and their perception suddenly became widened; learning became fun and later became the catalyst for widening their scope of perceiving things. The more learning became paramount in the lives of the people, the more vibrant the society became. Learning was the noble chariot of broadening this scope and was ushered in by leaders who came with vision and pragmatism.

I will also discuss the emergence of a new breed of leadership after the 20 years of war, which ushered in an era of political dialogue that brought down the rebellion peacefully and embarked on discerning areas of concern of the population. Emphasis on the introduction of educational institutions was the focus of the new leadership, and a challenge was set for those to continue with the banner of leadership, to water the seed so planted, to enable it bear fruit. The result was the explosion of education as the figures will show in this book.

This is in no way fiction or historical legend. It is the story of one young individual, who lived through it all, grew to become the youngest Member of Parliament in the central government of the Republic of Uganda and later left the scene unceremoniously. He lived to tell the story so that the next generation can **sieve** out lessons to be learned and to be told to the young people of this region.

In the later part of this narrative, we will see how twenty-five cents was significant in shaping the leadership style of this 26-year-old Member of Parliament. During the process of leaving the scene, after a humble 4 years in service, he was blessed with five US dollars which carried him to North America to live, settle, prosper and raise a family on hope, trusting in the mercies of the living God. At the end of this write up we will see the truth behind the myth unfold into reality and finally a kingdom of the people achieved.

Amos Mubunga Kambere

Chapter 1

On 30th of June, in the year of our Lord nineteen hundred and sixty-two, (1962) on a bright sunny Saturday afternoon, a declaration of independence was made by Isaya Mukirane, then leader of the Rwenzururu Movement. *A four-colored flag of blue for lakes, green for vegetation yellow for lowlands, and white for snow,* was hoisted at the headquarters of the Kingdom and an anthem already composed was sang by those who assembled to witness the occasion. The movement that included all the people of the mountain range constituted itself into an army of spears and sticks bearers, ready to liberate the entire mountain region from the leadership of the Toro Kingdom. Mr. Isaya Mukirane, the self-declared *President*, later became the King of the Kingdom after a declaration of secession from the Toro Kingdom, which was led by the *"Omukama Rukira Basaija"* of Toro. It is important to note here that the declaration of independence by Isaya came on 30th of June 1962; more than three months before Uganda acquired her own independence on October 9, 1962.

While Dr. Apollo Milton Obote was in London negotiating the instruments of independence for Uganda, the local leadership in the Toro Kingdom was behind closed doors embroidered in a constitutional crisis in which they had denied recognition of the Bakonzo and Bamba tribes as separate tribes in the constitution. The Rukurato [Toro parliament] had refused to include Lukonzo and Rwamba languages as languages that existed within the Kingdom.

The representatives of the Bakonzo and Bamba in this Rukurato had subsequently walked out of this unprecedented meeting. Among those who walked out of this Rukurato were Kawamara Yeremia, Peter Mupalia, Bazarabusa and Isaya Mukirane. Isaya later became the leader of the rebellion. A few of the Bakonzo representatives like Erisa Nzige did not walk out of the Rukurato. They were later made ministers in the Omukama's government in which the Bakonzo and Bamba were not recognized according to the constitution of Uganda which Dr. Obote carried with him to London to negotiate for Uganda's independence from the United Kingdom.

The Bakonzo and Bamba are the aborigines of the then Toro and it was inconceivable that they could be denied the right to exist in the Uganda constitution. This constitution stipulated that all people living in Toro district were Batoro.

Toro kingdom had been formed in 1830 by one Prince Olimi Kaboyo, who had rebelled against his father, the King of Bunyoro Kitara. This young rebel Prince had fled from Bunyoro to hide in the Mountains of the Moon which were inhabited by Bakonzo and Bamba. The Bakonzo had hidden this rebel King, whose heirs later turned against them and made them slaves. Despite the fact that all the inhabitants of Toro at the time were illiterate, all the available positions in the administration of the kingdom were to be given to Batoro when Toro was annexed to the British protectorate of Uganda by one Captain Lugard in 1893. The Bakonzo and Bamba became forced servants of the Batoro as a matter of policy. This caused much suffering and indignation among the Bakonzo and Bamba communities who made several attempts to liberate themselves. They staged a rebellion in 1919 led at this time by Nyamutswa, Tibamwenda and Kapoli. The Batoro leadership under the Omukama whose grandfather the Bakonzo had hidden in the mountain caves, arrested these three men, tortured them, and later killed them by hanging and burying them in one grave at Kagando, in Kisinga, the present site of Kagando Hospital.

Education and medical facilities were introduced in the Kingdom as I will discuss later in this book, but none were extended to Bakonzo and Bamba areas until the 1950s.

In 1961, the Bakonzo were allowed to send representatives to the Rukurato [Toro Parliament] and they used this chance to demand their inclusion in the Toro Constitution, which was rejected outright. When the matter was brought to the Governor General in Entebbe, the grievances were noted and confirmed as true. This caused more hatred between the Batoro and the Bakonzo- Bamba leaders forcing the latter to walk as it was useless to sit in a parliament whose constitution did not recognize their existence. This resulted in killings in large numbers of our people, and the whole of 1962 saw the counties of Busongora, Bwamba, Burahya and Bunyangabu declared as disturbed areas. This became the birth and entrenchment of the Rwenzururu Movement.

Chapter 2

July 10, 1962 was a busy Tuesday. It was a designated market day for the sub-county of Kyarumba where I was born. I was at that time in the market sitting beside my mother Julia who was selling banana juice [omubisi]. At about 12 noon, on that bright sunny day, about ten Rwenzururu soldiers armed with mere sticks arrived in the market and started hitting the ground with their sticks while shouting *"Rwenzururu, Rwenzururu, Rwenzururu"* in unison. The market vendors quickly dispersed and people took to their heels running for their lives. It had been common practice that if you heard men shouting the words "Rwenzururu", there was troubles to follow. These ten men expected people to reply in chorus as they shouted Rwenzururu. Failure to shout with them would result in being beaten up. Joining the chanting men was a sign of support for the declaration of independence, which had been announced two weeks earlier on 30 June, 1962. The Rwenzururu commanders at this time were targeting market places and churches on Sundays to send their message across. The declaration of independence by Isaya revitalized the morale of the Bakonzo and Bamba into a bitter struggle that was to last more than 20 years.

On that Tuesday, my mother and I left the juice unattended to and took off like every one else. As we fled, most of us had to join in the chorus of the Rwenzururu song to avoid retribution by the soldiers who could follow any direction. The trading center quickly came to a stand still and the local shops closed as the soldiers headed for the sub county [Gombolola] headquarters. The Chief at this sub-county was a Mutoro appointed by the Omukama of Toro. His name was Rwakijuma. The soldiers armed with sticks and pangas moved into the sub county headquarters, ransacked it and set the buildings on fire. The grass thatched ones around quickly vanished in flames while the permanent buildings were engulfed in smoke. Mr. Rwakijuma fled the scene and was never to be heard of again. He was believed to be armed with a rifle given to him by the Toro Kingdom assisted by the British who were still in charge as Uganda was not yet independent. It is interesting to note that Isaya declared Rwenzururu independent from Toro Kingdom before the entire Uganda became independent from the United Kingdom.

The uprising quickly spread throughout Bukonzo County. In Kisinga, on the following Friday, was a market day too. A different band of soldiers armed with spears and sticks arrived there, this time around mobilizing the Bakonzo from the market and marching towards the sub county [Gombolola] headquarters, which was some 300 meters away from the market. All in all, about 200 people marched towards the house of the gombolola chief, a Mutoro, with intentions of killing him and putting the house on fire. Not surprisingly this chief was armed with a shot gun. His name was Bamuloho. He fired through the window in self-defense, killing one of the Bakonzo demonstrators and managing to disperse the crowd. As they left the scene, they vandalized bridges, and torched Batoro houses as they fled back to the mountains shouting "Rwenzururu oye". These attacks spread in the entire region. On the side of the Toro area, the Batoro were attacking Bakonzo households in revenge and this caused an exodus of Bakonzo and Bamba and brought everything to a standstill. The following month saw the rebellion spread into Muhokya in Busongora. About 400 men armed with pangas and spears damaged property in the trading center and at the gombolola headquarters. During this riotous incident the police shot one Mukonzo.

Another group of Rwenzururu men infiltrated up to the omukama's palace. They were however apprehended before they made a disastrous move. One of the ideas they wanted to implement here was to infiltrate the enemy camp. They needed to outwit the enemy by mounting a solid intelligence from inside his own camp. This way they would have overrun the palace and taken it over; probably killing the "omukama" king.

These bands of people were not educated and basically depended on oral communications. Of course one cannot assume that they were retarded. Whether they used oral or written language their intelligence, cause and determination could not be underestimated or deterred.

While I could afford to miss school on a Tuesday morning to help my mother carry stuff to the market, I could not afford to be away on other days of the week. The following week I had to routinely go to school. As the disturbances raged on, some schools in the area were closed either because the teachers fled for their lives or some were simply arrested and could not perform their duties. Most of the teachers were Batoro just as were the chiefs. At this time the entire mountain region had been declared a disturbed area and a state of emergency had been declared. In February 1963 an elected member of the first parliament Mr. Ezironi Bwambale was picked up from Kinyamaseke as he was talking to farmers who had come to sell their cotton produce. Rwenzururu soldiers kidnapped him, took him uphill to Kabingo. When they could not carry him further up the hill, they stabbed him in the chest and left him in the valley either to die or to be rescued by the government troops who had immediately mounted a man search for him. Isaya Mukirane, the Rwenzururu president had ordered that Bwambale be brought before his council court to answer charges as to why he had decided to side with the Toro leadership and not introduced a motion in parliament seeking for a separate district for his people. Isaya still believed that a democratic process should have been followed to deal with the issues, which had led him, and his group to walk out of the "Rukurato". Bwambale was a member of the opposition Democratic Party [DP] that did not have a big say in the parliamentary decisions. Bwambale too, feared retribution from his constituency, which was largely dominated by Batoro voters who mostly lived on the lower lands of the mountain. Bwambale hailed from Bwera and most of his support was from Nyakatonzi, Katwe, Kilembe, Muhokya, Hima and Rwimi areas which had a large population of Batoro and most of whom were strong supporters of the Democratic Party, which sat on the opposition in the Uganda central government. Isaya accused Bwambale of not introducing a motion in parliament seeking the redress of the Bakonzo tribal issues. Isaya did not realize that Bwambale had just been elected, and had not even made his maiden speech in parliament moreover he was on the opposition.

Eventually Bwambale was rescued by helicopter; alive bleeding and was taken to Kilembe mines hospital for treatment until the ministry of internal affairs ordered his transfer to Mulago hospital in Kampala. He was transported by police helicopter. At this point the Bakonzo and Bamba were dominated by sadness, deep frustrations as they asked questions why their basic human rights were being violated even by the central government, for which they had sent an elected Mukonzo from which they thought solace would come. The infrastructure had broken down; schools and health centers had closed down. With the kidnapping and consequently the stabbing of a Member of Parliament, the Prime Minister, Dr. A Milton Obote had no choice other than declaring the Rwenzururu secessionist movement to be a "dangerous movement to peace and order".

The Prime Minister and the Governor-General were quoted in the Uganda Argus, the government newspaper of February 18, 1963 as saying "the Rwenzururu movement has disgraced Uganda in the eyes of the world". Indeed as disturbances increased unabated, it was increasingly clear that the central government was failing to bring the rebellion to an end. This grossly hampered the delivery of services to the people. However, the Rwenzururu leadership and the people who now entirely supported the movement did not care about services especially when they knew that the Toro Kingdom government was violating their human rights. The Bakonzo and Bamba had vowed that it is better to perish than live in slavery. This was the guiding principle that kept the fire burning in all Rwenzururu-dominated areas. The central government, in their own desperation were scared that the situation was getting out of hand. They wanted to recapture their image in the eyes of the international community.

At this point they allowed Mr. Tom Stacey, a British writer and journalist who had written a few books about the mountains of the moon and the Rwenzururu movement, to come and meet with the Rwenzururu King. The central government now had to depend on Mr. Stacey to salvage their image by probably convincing Mukirane to abandon the rebellion and surrender. Mr. Stacey was able to meet with Isaya Mukirane in February 1963. He was the first negotiator appointed by the Ugandan government to attempt to end the movement, but his mission failed miserably and Isaya and his leadership moved further in the mountains in what was considered as the "furthest private cave".

Tom Stacey

The central government had deployed heavily by sending two companies of the Uganda Rifles who were already moving into the mountains with the help of local porters. As they moved about the mountains they were burning Bakonzo huts, houses and destroying property in a bid to cut off communication between the local Bakonzo and the Rwenzururu leadership.

Mr. Tom Stacey became a frequent visitor to the mountains because he had developed a personal relationship with the Rwenzururu people and their leadership. On most occasions he was mistakenly called "Isemusoki" a name which was given to another white man, who worked in Bwamba. Isemusoki, the husband to Nyamusoki lives in Norway while Kirstern Alnaes – Nyamusoki lives in London. This couple lived and worked extensively in Bwamba, had their first born baby girl after consulting a local medicine man in Bwamba who told them to name their first child Musoki if she was a girl. Because she lived with the Bamba for a long time and wrote books about the cultures of the Bakonzo and Bamba, she became famous. So when Tom Stacey returned to the Rwenzoris, the Bakonzo not knowing the difference between white people [*muzungus*] just called him Isemusoki. In the mean time, the leadership of the Rwenzururu, called him "Musabuli" which meant savior, because they liken him to "Jesus who came to save sinner". The fact that a white man could come all the way from London and side with the cause of the Bakonzo and Bamba was equivalent to being a savior, hence the name of Musabuli. One of the factors about Tom which impressed the Mukirane leadership was that as he traveled through the mountains, he knew where the army deployments were and was able to give warning to Bakonzo natives of the dangers that were coming along. He was also able to tell the Rwenzuru leadership of how they were being sought by the advancing army. This enabled them to move into their furthest private cave. Today, this Tom Stacey has remained a 'legend' or is he, among the Bakonzo people. He is still accorded the dignity of a Musabuli especially when people think of his initiative to bring to the attention of the central government the plight of the Banyarwenzururu. Mr. Stacey's mission failed simply because he came from a democracy and when he heard the plight of the Bakonzo, read copies of their several memoranda to the government, he could not then ask them to surrender. He quickly grasped their concept of human rights violation, he grieved with them and instead of becoming a negotiator, and he became an ally. In March 1963 after Tom Stacey had failed to bring the rebellion to reasonable understanding with the government, a white paper was issued recognizing what the commission of inquiry had recommended… "That seceding from Toro by the Bakonzo and Bamba was not acceptable". The white paper reaffirmed the emergency measures to continue until law and order was re-established. The white paper says "the Government realizes that its decisions will not satisfy the *'extreme demands'* of some Bakonzo and Bamba who want to secede from Toro and establish a separate district. But it trusts that these tribes and the people of Toro and the Omukama's government will loyally accept the central government's decisions". [Uganda Argus march26, 1963] For the government white paper to refer to us as "these tribes" while referring to the Batoro as the "people of Toro" clearly indicated that the government condoned the gross violation of the human rights of our people. Therefore there was necessary cause to be part of the rebellion.

This assertion by the central government that the Bakonzo were demanding for a separate district dispels claims and accusations that Isaya Mukirane had declared independence for the Rwenzuru as a "state". It was a mere declaration of independence from the Toro Kingdom and a demand for a separate district in which services could be equitably distributed to serve the entire population.

It had been common practice that under the Toro Kingdom government, the Bakonzo and Bamba were sidelined, denied any possible employment in the Omukama's government and bursaries for Education were not extended to people who came from the Rwenzururu dominated areas. A commission of inquiry appointed by the Governor General led by Dr. Sembeguya found out that the Omukama's government in Toro had instituted discrimination and bias as a matter of policy. The Sembeguya report had recommended that "at the general election, Toro should not prevent anybody who was truly representative from standing for elections". It further recommended that the "present leaders of the Rwenzururu must be permitted to return to Toro and stand for election". However, this was not acceptable to the Toro leadership because the Batoro had a tendency of treating Bakonzo and Bamba as inferior and less than human beings. The Sembeguya commission was told of the abusive and arrogant behavior directed by the Batoro to the Bakonzo and Bamba in which Batoro officials called us "apes, gorillas, baboons, dogs, insects, flies and pigs". This was the underlying evidence to confirm why the Batoro refused to include the names of Bamba and Bakonzo in the Toro agreement. The commission urged the Toro government to announce publicly that the three main tribes in the kingdom were Batoro, Bakonzo and Bamba, but the Omukama's government blatantly refused to heed this recommendation, fueling more troubles among the opposing tribes. When the Toro government admitted that the Bakonzo and Bamba areas were **educationally under developed**, the commission recommended "that special arrangements should be made to eliminate the disparity". The report recommended that for five years, funds supplied for bursaries be devoted to the Bakonzo and Bamba students in order to alleviate the disparity in Education. This however, because of discrimination and bias, was never implemented and the Rwenzori area remained behind in all sectors of development. With all these in mind, the movement's rebellion spread all over the Rwenzuru area and attracted more sympathies than condemnation.

In all this, the central government was ambivalent about the whole scenario. The Parliament in Kampala while debating the introduction of a state of emergency in the Rwenzuru area, had the guts to listen to members of the Democratic Party who formed the opposition, that the Bakonzo and Bamba people be moved by the army to another area so that their homeland may be declared into a National Park. This proposal was presented on the floor of parliament by DP Member of Parliament, the Hon. F. Kangwamu from Ankole South-East constituency. Thanks to UPC Minister Hon. Flex Onama who said, "There is no DP, UPC, Protestant, Catholic, in the minds of Bakonzo and Bamba, only Rwenzururu". He was echoing what one of the leaders Mr. Kawamara had said earlier in his statement to the government that, "nothing can be gained by ordering the Uganda Rifles to arrest anybody they simply suspect of being Rwenzururu supporter; everyone who lived in those counties was regarded as a rwenzururian, whether he believes in it or not". It is inconceivable to believe that the Bakonzo and Bamba could still vote the Democratic Party leadership despite the motion moved by a DP member of parliament to have the entire tribe moved and their God given land declared as a national park for animals. In spite of this, it was an uphill task for the Uganda Peoples' Congress [UPC] to penetrate their campaign in the Ruwenzori. This in part was because at that time the political parties were run based on religions. The fact that the majority of the inhabitants were Catholics; it was a foregone conclusion that they would support the democratic party regardless of what DP members said about them in parliament. This goes as well, to explain why they have gone to vote for politically-disoriented people with less developmental ideas as long as they are Catholics.

Chapter 3

While the bickering about the security situation in the Rwenzori was going on in parliament, the movement was getting entrenched among all the inhabitants of the mountains of the moon. The army was continuing to arrest and torture persons they suspected of supporting the movement. Houses were being torched and school and health centers were getting deserted since most employees were Batoro and were no longer welcome to work under the movement government. A tax policy had been introduced and Isaya Mukirane's government was now functional both in principle and in practice. Those who refused to subscribe by paying the 'nzururu' tax had to leave the area. Some people opted to pay two taxes, that of the Omukama for fear of retribution by the Uganda army and that of Isaya Mukirane's government for fear of blame by the rest of the Bakonzo who were paying willingly. Despite non-compliance by the Bakonzo for the central government's laws and orders, one of theirs Mr. Timothy Bazarabusa was nominated to represent the Bakonzo in the legislative Council, the "*Legico*" as a back bencher.

During the general election of 1961 DP candidate, Ezironi Bwambale, defeated Mr.Bazarabusa. However, because Bazarabusa was an effective member of the Legico and personally know to the Prime Minister, Dr. Apollo Milton Obote, he was appointed Uganda's first High Commissioner to Britain. This would have been considered a great honor that Obote gave to the Bakonzo, to pick one of theirs to occupy that high office despite the tribal war that was raging on. Dr Obote clearly knew that the Bakonzo did not support his party because they refused to vote for Bazarabusa. By voting for Bwambale of the DP, the Bakonzo were sending a clear message that they would not support the government of Prime Minister Milton Obote. However, Obote did not buy into this; he went an extra mile and appointed a Mukonzo to what was considered the highest office in the foreign affairs ministry.

WHO WAS THIS TIMOTHY BAZARABUSA?

Bazarabusa was the son of one mukonzo [*munyangetse*] called Paulo Byabasakuzi. Byabasakuzi and his wife were among some of the first Bakonzo families who were taken to Kabarole as slaves to the Omukama. He escaped from the kingdom bondage and followed Apolo Kibavulaya, the missionary who brought religion to the mountain land. Byabasakuzi traveled as far as Rwanda and Mboga Zaire [Congo] helping this missionary in his bid to spread Christianity. He later became the first run away slave to train as a church catechist. Timothy Bazarabusa growing up with palace connections benefited from the palace education facilitation. He was one of the few people from the Toro Kingdom who went to Makerere Collage as early as 1934 to obtain a diploma in Education. He served as a headmaster of Kabarole primary school, a position which could not be given to a mukonzo unless you had palace connections. Because of his love for education and his contributions, he was awarded the prestigious order of the British Empire by Governor Sir Andrew Cohen. As a man, he settled in Kasisi, a village near the royal palace. He then married a lady from the Babito clan, the royal clan. This *'Mubitokati'* Caroline gave birth to two girls before she died at an early age. Bazarabusa, then widowed, married a Muganda lady, Jane the daughter of Kulubya, the first African Mayor of Kampala.

Bazarabusa did not forget where his family had come from. He used his office as Native Anglican Church schools supervisor to advocate for building schools in his homeland. While he was working hard to advocate for education in his home area, he was nominated to the "*Legico*", the Legislative Council as backbencher representing Toro Kingdom. The Governor, Sir Andrew Cohen had seen in Bazarabusa exceptional leadership quality that no other African had displayed. In 1959 he had served on the constitutional committee, "the Wild Committee" where his contributions to the future of Uganda's independence has been noticed by Milton Obote of the Uganda Peoples' Congress.

Prime Minister Apollo Milton Obote later appointed him as the first Uganda High Commissioner to the United Kingdom. The appointment to this office did not please the Omukama's government and was received with impunity by the Batoro loyalists. It remained the highest political appointment the Bakonzo and Bamba had ever received and remained so until 1986 when a full cabinet minister was appointed from those tribes.

Bazarabusa the senior diplomat was recalled to came home for consultation towards the end of 1965 as the government cabinet was deciding on constitutional matters that would evolve Uganda into a republican state. During this time he went around the Rwenzori visiting schools. It is generally believed that during these constultations, he had strong feelings for Kingdoms as he had grown out of the Toro kingdom and was even married to princese. His second wife too was from the Buganda kingdom hierachy. Bazarabusa did not celebrate the following year's independence and did not see the republican constitution launched. On April 25, 1966 Bazarabusa, the top diplomat was found dead in his car, a Volkswagen that had been driven under a bus. The engine of this car is usually behind and it is said that it was still running while the front was stuck underneath the bus. Whether this was the work of '*Batoro bad elements*' in Kampala, or political rivilary among the national cabinet or just an accident, has never been known to date, and will probably never be known. There was no inquiry into this death, and it appears there will never be.

Chapter 4

Bazarabusa, as schools supervisor in the Omukama's government used this office to build schools in the mountain areas of the Rwenzori. Some of the schools he helped set up that are still standing today include Nyamisule, Nkangi Mahango, Bukangama, Kabingo, and Ihandiro primary schools. Most of these schools were built with corrugated iron sheets. The enrolment in these schools was very high but the graduates from them did not receive bursaries and/or scholarships from the Toro government as mentioned earlier. When the army moved into the mountain areas hunting for Isaya Mukirane, the schools closed. Most of the teachers fled the areas for fear of revenge because majority of them were Batoro.

In spite of all this backwardness and under development, the people of the Rwenzori remained resilient with a strong hope that one-day favor will come their way. It was not easy at this point to destroy their cause.

In 1963 when I was in grade school, Mr. Bazarabusa came to our school, Kyarumba primary school. He was on a tour to celebrate with the Bakonzo as he was going to take up a senior job as Uganda's High Commissioner to UK. We sang songs for him and while on parade, he asked my headmaster, Mr. Bahindi, a mutoro at that time to allow him to inspect the students. When he came to my line he spotted me, and said to me, "You are a very smart, well dressed boy. How old are you?" When I told him I was eight [8] years of age, he smiled and reached into his pocket and gave me twenty five cents. I have never forgotten this moment. This was the first time I ever saw him and was also the last. The people of the Rwenzori will never forget the contribution he made towards the development of education in this area. The sprouting of education in this region makes me echo the biblical passage in 1Corinthians 3:6 which reads, "***I sowed the seed, Apollos watered the plant, but it was God who made the plant grow. The one who sows and the one who waters really do not matter. It is God who matters, because he makes the plant grow.***" This is exactly what had sustained the hopes and aspirations of the Bakonzo and Bamba in achieving their education goals. This biblical analogy strengthened the hopes and faith of the people and as those buildings remain standing, it will take a long time to forget the promotion of education which Bazarabusa initiated. The schools he helped build in his bid to promote education are like a seed he planted, and the 25 cents he gave me is the equivalent of a bucket of water he gave me to water the seed. I did not know that 20 years down the road I would jump into Bazarabusa's shoes to advocate for the building of more schools at all levels in order to boost our educational capacity, as I will discuss in later chapters.

As the youngest Member of Parliament ever elected in Uganda, at 26 years of age, I did not have much on my political manifesto, except to recognize that my people were educationally backward, and that the best way forward was to advocate and promote education above all issues. My primary task was to convince the population that education was the best weapon to fight backwardness, poverty, repression and enslavement. At the time Bazarabusa left the scene, backwardness, poverty, and deep frustration dominated the people of the Rwenzori. The people here were the least educated in the Toro Kingdom. The schools Bazarabusa helped to build produced students with brilliant results. But they could not go beyond junior secondary school level. The first junior secondary school which could take graduates from all primary six schools in the entire Rwenzori was Bwera Junior Secondary School, opened in 1958. Most bright Bakonzo and Bamba were advised to go to teachers' colleges instead of pursuing higher education. Besides, there would be no bursaries for them if they opted to go further. During these early days, it was not possible for anyone to go to Kings College Budo, Namiliango College, St. Mary's Kisubi, Nyakasura, Ntare, Namagunga or Gayaza secondary schools. Mr. Karugaba Selvesta was the first headmaster of Bwera Junior Secondary school in 1958. He was succeeded by Mr. Samwiri Mutoro, the first Rwenzori native to head the highest institution of learning in the Rwenzoris at that time.

Samwiri Mutoro was so innovative that after Karugaba, he initiated a program of Bakonzo and Bamba students looking beyond teacher education and pursuing higher education. He had been a member of the Bakonzo Life History Research Society started by Isaya Mukirane. He was a famous Mathematics and Religious Knowledge teacher. I remember one of his students who became my primary six teacher, Mr. Uliya Baluku telling us in class that the best way to memorize the names of the North American great lakes as taught by Samuiri Mutoro was by simply saying "**S**amwiri **M**utoro **H**as **E**aten **O**ranges". It is so funny that even in today's North American teaching; they have similar colloquial acronyms for memorizing the famous great lakes. For them in North America they use "**HOMES**" with each letter representing each one of the Great Lakes.

Mr. Samwiri B. Mutooro

Samwiri Mutoro being one of the most highly educated citizens of the Rwenzoris opted to join politics as a member of the Uganda Peoples

Congress and ran for office in 1962. He lost to the Democratic Party candidate, Mr. Ezron Bwambale. The UPC party fielded two candidates at the time while the DP had one candidate. In fact both Samwiri and Bazarabusa were very valuable candidates. But Dr. Obote chose to have Bazarabusa. Mr.Samwiri Mutoro later opted to go to North America to study Theology in a Montreal Christian college. He died by motor accident on the way to Fort Portal after returning from Canada. During the short period Mutoro was away from Bwera Junior Secondary School, another dynamic Mukonzo, who later became a Music scholar; Semu AbwoliKiyonga briefly headed the school until 1966. At this time the junior secondary schools were abolished by legislation. Mr. Blasio Maate took over the school as it became a primary school, still regarded as the best in the Rwenzoris, producing candidates to join Secondary Schools; this time with more focus on higher education and no longer teacher education as was the case during the Karugaba years. Some schools in Toro which were Junior Schools were phased out and automatically became secondary schools, but the Ruwenzori ones only became primary schools. Was this pre-planned not to have secondary schools as junior schools were being phased out? This could be partly attributed to weak representation in parliament at the time legislation was introduced to abolish junior secondary schools. With effective representation, Rwenzori would have had two secondary schools by promoting Bwera and Nsenyi junior schools to secondary. They were however both demoted to primary schools.

Following the Sembeguya Commission Report, government had set up a desk in the office of the District Education Officer to oversee the schools in Bwamba and Busongora. The first person in charge of this desk was one Mr. Nantamu all the way from Busoga. By this time the Native Anglican Church had surrendered the administration of schools to the government as the UPC sought to end the relationship between religion and politics. Nantamu tried his best to improve on the existing schools. His work was complicated by the on going war between the Batoro and Isaya Mukirane's rebel militia. After Nantamu, we had Rwatsika and later Rucecerwa; all serving as Education

Officers, but very little is known about their major contributions towards education in the area other than purely administrative. What I remember about them especially Mr. Ruchecherwa was for him to visit schools that wanted an extension of a classroom. Whenever a school wanted to move on to the next grade, the education officer or the inspector of schools as they were called at that time came to see whether the school should have an additional class. In most cases they looked at the enrolment and the potential for expansion. Pupils were called to parade. The education official inspected the parade by walking along each line which represented each class. This was the best way they could ascertain the number of pupils per class; carrying out a head count. They did not want to go by the register, because sometimes some pupils were not registered either because they did not pay fees or simply were not available during registration. A physical head count on the parade was the best way to know the school enrolment. The other reason why they insisted on parade was because most of the teachers and head teachers at the time were not qualified. The qualified Batoro had left due to the insurgency and the schools were left to be manned by untrained people. The pupils were ill trained below accepted standards for many years. For example in English most teachers were as 'green' as the pupils they taught. For example during school band performance which happened on every market day, the whole school with teachers alike could go on singing a song in what sounded like English for many years without knowing what the actual pronunciations of the words were and the meaning of the song. Here is a typical example of one common song which was sung by most if not all the schools in the school band: "**oh John wazeverio.ooh oooh John wazeverio-... John friend mayi**" This was sang by many students and even as late as July 2006 one such former student in those schools now living in the United States did not know what that song was except to continue telling his children that they used to sing "oh john wazeverio..." during parades and school bands. When I actually told that father of six children what the song should have been, he was almost hysterical to see what kind of injustice he went through as he struggled to earn his education. The song actually was:

"oh John was a warrior, ooh oooh John was warrior; John French man." The intention of the song was to teach the pupils to match like John who was a warrior and a French man during the Second World War. School bands instilled discipline among pupils. That is why the education systems allowed it in their school curriculum.

Dr. Apollo Milton Obote, MP

Now came the general elections of 1962 and the politicians of both the Democratic Party and the Uganda Peoples Congress were scrambling about trying to cajole the people into voting for them. At this time, the Uganda People's Congress fielded Mr. Samuiri Mutooro, a teacher and an educational reformer. This was a man who would have taken over Bazarabusa's job even more effectively. He however lost the election to Mr. Bwambale a second time. Again the DP candidate prevailed. These two elections of 1961 and 1962 signified that UPC was unpopular among the Bakonzo and Bamba people. This was greatly due to the fact that Prime Minister Obote, who was the leader of the UPC, did not grant the request Isaya had put across, which was, separation from the Toro Kingdom. The issue of separate districts had been discussed in the Legislative council and the motion had been defeated. Of course, Prime Minister Obote could not unliterary order for the creation of separate districts, when parliament had voted no. He was strictly observing the principle of ruling by consensus. Prime

Minister Obote believed in parliamentary democracy and could not become dictatorial just for the sake of the Bamba and Bakonzo people. This however, was not appreciated by Isaya's movement, and therefore the struggle continued with more tension mounting in all over the Rwenzoris.

Dr. Milton Obote had the intellectual stimulation of dealing with difficult political issues, but he was dealing with a national assembly that had a member of the opposition representing the disturbed area. I believe he missed the despondency of not being able to come up with answers, which gave him very little emotional reward. The people in the Rwenzoris would have loved to see Dr. Obote act unliterary against the Batoro and this would have opened a window for any UPC candidate to win in an election in the Rwenzururu areas. The people in the Rwenzoris voted for the Democratic Party of Ben Kiwanuka. This is the only time they were able to side with the Omukama's government by voting alongside their traditional foes.

Chapter 5

The whole of 1963 saw the Rwenzuru rebellion intensified and the entire mountain range was on fire. The army had moved in and camped on mountain tops because they feared rolling stones; one of the weapons of the Bakonzo fighters. Stone rolling had been proved effective in the Bwamba region and was being used in the Bukonzo and Busongora areas as well.

The Uganda Argus of February 21, 1963 reported that "One police constable was hit on the face by rolling stones and received stitches". This happened when police went to investigate an incident in Bwamba village. A mob of Bamba people attacked the police with rolling stones and got away with it. This kind of insecurity became rampant in the rest of the mountain area. Public and essential services came to a stand still. School and health centers were closed. All injuries were taken either to Kabarole hospital or Kilembe Mines hospital.

My headmaster, Mr. Bahindi had been attacked by a mob of Rwenzururu soldiers and had fled to Toro... never to return. A caretaker headmaster was appointed to head the Kyarumba primary school. This was now the only school that was open. It only runs up to primary six. Graduates from this school had to travel all the way to Bwera to join the junior school, others traveled to Nsenyi Junior Secondary School. These were the highest institutions of learning in the Kasese and Bundibugyo districts for a long time. At least during the disturbances, one school in each sub county remained open. Most of these schools had to be on the lower lands in order for them to receive protection from the central government. The Toro government was not bothered about the closures of schools because their own schools were running. When Batoro teachers left our areas, they were quickly deployed to teach in schools in other parts of the Toro kingdom. In 1964, while we were in class, an attempt was made to close our school too. A group of 6 Rwenzururu soldiers armed with sticks descended on the school. They surrounded the small building that housed class five and six. Mr. Yofesi Tembo was acting headmaster and also teaching in the grade five classroom. He was dragged out of the class, beaten with sticks across his chest and across his back before his students. These six revolutionary young fighters besieged the class. We were in the lower building of the school and when we saw what was happening, we jumped through the windows and fled for our lives. The teachers too in these buildings fled instead of coming to the aid of their colleague. Mr. Tembo with a bunch of other grade two teachers were about the highest qualified personnel in the Bukonzo and Bwamba counties. They were determined to keep the schools in the region opened. We did not have grade three teachers at this time. While most of the resources for development came from the Bukonzo area like the taxes from the Katwe salt lake, the taxes from the Kilembe Mines, the sale of coffee and cotton, taxes from the tourist industry attracted by Queen Elizabeth National Park to name but a few. The authorities in Fort Portal did not mind developing the region from where they received most of their revenue in taxes. Most development took place in the Toro area. During the colonial time under the Omukama's government, schools were built to cater for the entire Toro Kingdom, but all of them were built in Toro, a simple sign that Rwenzori was just not considered part of the Toro Kingdom; this being one of the factors that made Isaya intensify his rebellion. Nyakasura *[commonly referred to as the school]* one of the oldest schools in Uganda was built in the Toro area, including Butiti Teachers College, Canon Apollo teachers college, Kicwamba Technical College, St. Leos College Kyegobe, Mpaga High School, and Kyebambe Girls' Secondary school. These educational institutions were all concentrated within ten [10] kilometers of each other. To make matters worse, for a Mukonzo to be admitted in these institutions, you either had to change your name and sound like you are a Mutoro or you had to completely change your personality and become a Mutoro. Unfortunately even if you changed your personality or name to become a Mutoro, you could never claim land ownership on Toro land. This irregularity in the education sector went on almost until 1980. People used to hide their personalities and pretend to belong to either a certain clan or tribe that was associated with the powers that was. A lot of our brilliant people who had passed very well after their junior secondary school from Bwera and Nsenyi could not be admitted to these institutions. The lucky ones ended up going to Kakoba Teachers College, and a few who managed to beat the system ended up going to Kampala's Day Schools or Private Schools. Bakonzo and Bamba students who had names that sounded like Byabasaija, Tibaijuka, Bagarukayo, Kobusinge, Katuramum, Byabagambe, Kobujune, Byaruhanga, Mbabazi, Baguma etc found favor with the Toro Education Authority. I am a living testimony to this because my parents had given me a middle name as Tibaijuka so that I could navigate with ease as my first job was to teach at Kyebambe girls' school in Toro district. Imagine and compare the two junior schools we had in Kasese and none in Bwamba to the many I mentioned earlier, situated in Fort Portal. It was unbelievable that in spite of all the educational injustice, we had a small group of *elite* who managed to educate the generation that followed. The issue of scholarships and bursaries was unheard of when it came to students from Kasese and Bwamba. One of the earliest graduates from Bukonzo is Dr. Barnabas Rwatooro [RIP]. Does his name of Rwatoro ring any bells? He was the first Mukonzo to graduate from Makerere University with a medical degree in 1967. Since independence in 1962, up till 1967, Toro Kingdom had several graduates, while the Banyarwenzururu saw their first, only in 1967.

The first female graduate was Bonabana Kitakakire Candida in 1972 from Makerere University, Kampala. Does her name of Bonabana ring any bells? She got a Bachelor of Social Work and Social Administration [SWASA]. She went to Nsenyi Primary, Mary Hill in

Mbarara and Trinity College Nabbingo. If you consider the rest of the Toro Kingdom, lots of graduates in various field were in abundance even as early as 1960 before Uganda earned her independence. Between 1960 and 1967 there were zero graduate in the Bakonzo and Bamba areas.

In the Department of Agriculture, we did not have a qualified agricultural officer to advise our peasants on agricultural methods. The highest qualified agricultural officer was Mr. Paul Nzobindo in 1968 with just a Diploma in agriculture. The Bukonzo area was one of the highest producers of maize, coffee, cotton and other substance crops. While our people just used their own crude method of farming to produce for a living; our students who would have gone to school to specialize in Agriculture were not given the motivation and encouragement from the Toro Education Authority. Most of our young men and women were encouraged to take up teaching at grade two level, although these were just the lucky ones. The Bukonzo and Busongora counties were famous for the production of copper and salt. Both of these commodities earned plenty of revenue in taxes to the Toro government, but there were no kickbacks injected in the Bakonzo economy. All the wealth was concentrated in the Kabarole areas to develop the Omukama's "favorite territory". Busongora County was famous for the production of fish and a booming industry was placed on Lake George, at Kasenyi called "The Uganda Fish Marketing African Corporation" [TUFMAC]. You could not find a qualified Mukonzo or Mwamba working in this fishing industry. Our people only provided casual and manual labor. Most of them were termed group employees. This merely meant that we provided unskilled labor. Why, because we were not educated enough to sit in comfortable positions within the fish plant, but there were Batoro and other 'gentlemen' from other tribes who were well educated, some of them as fisheries officers with degrees, diplomas and certificates working in and around the lakes in the Bakonzo land. Some people often argue that Ugandans are free to work anywhere as long as there was work. But the point I am making here is that even at a local level at Kasenyi, we could not find a native from the

Bakonzo land who had even a certificate to be able to work along with other Ugandans. Besides, we did not have any Mukonzo or Mwamba working elsewhere in Uganda, if we have to argue that Ugandans are free to work anywhere as long as there is work and are qualified to do so. This brought imbalance in opinion, generating disaffection especially when it came allocation of resources for development. It was ironical that even with the factory on Lake George, at Kasenyi, a decent primary school was never constructed to cater for the surrounding population. Little wonder, everybody who worked there did not have their families there, so they did not have feelings for the people who were providing them with local manpower and food, by thinking and working towards putting up a decent school for the kids. They had no kids of their own to go into the school because better schools were already in place where they hailed from. If they ever did, however, it would not please the Omukama of Toro because, then the local people would go to this school, get education and have their eyes open to see the injustice that was going on within the Kingdom leadership. The omukama feared challenge from educated people. If you take the example of Kilembe Mines - copper was being mined from the ground, under people's homes. No notice was ever given to indigenous people that pipes would be passing under their homes or hills, and therefore no proposal was made as to having a financial benefit from the industry. Schools were built by the mine authorities especially so because the management was by Canadian expatriates who were obligated to build schools for their children. The kids of the natives were not allowed in these schools unless their parents worked in the mines. What is funny here is that even the manual laborers who worked underground the mines came from as far as Kabale and Kabarole. One can argue that maybe the Bakonzo were unwilling to work in the mines, but this is not true. What is true is that with very little education, it was general knowledge that they could not fit-in into the work force where the administrative structures were managed by foreigners. The Batoro and Bakiga fitted in because they had some basic education and their children benefited by attending these mines schools. However, in spite of all these cases, Isaya Mukirane and his team had seen all the injustice and were busy calling upon all the Bakonzo and Bamba to follow and support the demand for a separate kingdom in order that the Bakonzo might be able to administer their own resources. Isaya had whipped up the support of a large number of peasants who formed the majority of the population. The middle class, if there was any at this time, was a little ambivalent about the ambitions of the proclaimed "king", although their fears were put to rest as the struggle progressed. As the fighting raged on, so was the hatred between the Bakonzo and the Batoro. Skirmishes between these groups of people continued on both the Bwamba side and the Bukonzo/Busongora side of the Omukama' Kingdom. One of the issues I believe Prime Minister Milton Obote did not want to consider was the creation of another Kingdom, because he was already planning to get rid of Kingdoms and declare Uganda a Republic. In 1966, the Uganda Peoples' Congress, UPC came up with the republican constitution in which all Kingdoms were to be dissolved or were they to be abolished? In 1967 Dr. Obote became the President of Uganda and dropped the post of Prime Minister. There were changes in the central government; however, these did not affect the Rwenzuru Kingdom. Isaya Mukirane had insisted earlier that his kingdom could not be abolished together with the rest of the Kingdoms because in the first place it was not recognized under the 1962 independence constitution. "We neither had a kingdom or a district. This Kingdom was self-proclaimed and self-independent by June 30, 1962". Isaya Mukirane together with the people, who lived around the Rwenzoris and supported him, had constituted themselves into "an independent kingdom" opposed to the Toro Kingdom and sought from the central government to separate from the Toro Kingdom. Both the demands for a Kingdom or a district had been denied by the powers that were in place. This is exactly why the war of the Rwenzururu did not end. The entire tribes of the Bakonzo, Basongora, Banyabindi, Bamba, Batuku and Babulebule, were dissatisfied with the leadership at the time and unanimously agreed to continue to fight until separation was achieved. The only umbrella under which they could all fit while fighting for their human rights was the "Rwenzururu umbrella" under the leadership of "king" Isaya Mukirane. Some people have even up till today interpreted the declaration of independence by Isaya as declaration of state sovereignty. Historian Dr. Arthur Syahuka-Muhindo, in The Rwenzururu Movement and the Democratic Struggle says; *"in general terms, this attitude which was initiated by Kaboyo as the founder of the Toro State caused class misalignment right from the start of the Kingdom. Dominant local classes were subordinated to largely alien ones in the power structure of Toro Kingdom. This encouraged more Balisa, Basita, and Bahinda clans to migrate to Toro to consolidate and benefit from Babito rule there. The political consequence of this process was the erosion of power and freedom for the Baamba and Bakonzo as a people. ...The Toro establishment was resisted by local dominant classes because of the nature of its organization and its political orientation. The chiefs of Busongora and Bukonzo vehemently resisted the new rule."* [p284].

As Prof. Syahuka Muhindo further contends, "kingdoms or settlements south of Lake George were generally referred to as States." It was therefore a misconstrued idea to refer to the Rwenzururu Kingdom as a sovereign state. This was not Isaya's intention because even Isaya's close associates like Mupalya and Kawamara who on many occasions led delegations to meet with the central government leadership, talked of separate district and not 'state'. Although politicians from opposing opinions floated ideas that Rwenzururu was created to establish a Rwenzururu state, records will show that this was not true. The Bakonzo/Bamba intended to secede from Toro Kingdom as it were. In the document signed by Isaya, Kawamara and Mupalya during the declaration of independence in June 1962, the trio after reiterating the grievances for the Bamba/Bakonzo against Batoro closed their document by saying:

*"Now let us all be in wait, no brutality, nor torture shall make us ever plead for mercy, for we prefer peace and freedom of speech in an **independent Uganda** to malicious Batoro Government. Long live Uganda.* Uhuru!" [p298]

Historians have recorded that "when the Bakonzo/Bamba leaders learned that the Toro Constitutional Committee members were going to leave for Entebbe without their representatives, they decided to send a Bakonzo Bamba party too. ... It was at this dramatic meeting with the Governor on February 26, 1962 that Mukirane, as the leader of the Bamba/Bakonzo delegation handed to him the memorandum which demanded a separate district for the Bamba/Bakonzo".[p296]. It is therefore; inconceivable for any sober minded leader to think of statehood around the Ruwenzori's when the original leaders did not conceive that idea of statehood. Mukirane made several attempts to send delegations to OAU and the United Nations, but failed constantly. He wanted the plight of the Bakonzo and Bamba to be heard by higher authorities, those that would sympathize with our human right situation and put pressure on the central government to listen to the Rwenzururu grievances. Isaya Mukirane continued with his vision to liberate the Bakonzo and Bamba from the tyranny inflicted upon them by their oppressors, the Omukama's Batoro people. Isaya was a mere Grade Two teacher who was not even accorded the privilege of being a headmaster of a primary school. He had only been elected to represent the Bakonzo Bamba in the Toro parliament out of which he had walked when the Toro parliament refused a resolution to include the Bakonzo and Bamba and the Lukonzo and Rwamba languages in the Toro Agreement. The Toro parliament had succeeded in making sure that the Bakonzo/Bamba do not receive recognition as part of Ugandan society. Isaya together with other movement leaders also challenged the motion put forward by Samson Rusoke, the last Omuhikirwa [Prime Minister] of the Toro Kingdom, which declared that "only a Mutoro Nyakabara shall be Katikiro of Toro" in 1962. According to Dr. Arthur Syahuka Muhindo, "a mutooro Nyakabara means 'a proper or Real Mutoro – that one whose origin is Babito" p284. This notion was discriminatory and was meant to eliminate any Mukonzo or Mwamba who would aspire to become Katikiro. Such qualities had been seen in Isaya and other bakonzo leaders like Timothy Bazarabusa and Yeremiya Kawamara. To the Omukama's parliament, all Bakonzo were to be considered Batoro and there would be no language called Lukonzo, therefore this would give room for anybody to aspire for the powerful post of Katikiro. The Batoro were further intimidated by the qualities they had seen in the Rwenzururu leaders so they made sure that they remained in jail during the National Parliamentary elections which would have probably returned them to a National parliament, where they could have aired their view to a more understanding forum. Because the Bakonzo and Bamba lacked representation in the Omukama's government, when it came to development, and distribution of services, priority was given to the Batoro, and if anything remained on the budget; then it would spill over to the Rwenzoris. To Isaya and his colleagues, who included Mr. Bulasio Maate, this was ridiculously unacceptable and had to be resisted by force even if it meant the entire tribe perishing. One other factor which infuriated the Bakonzo and Bamba according to Authur Syahuka-Muhindo was the fact that Isaya, Kawamara and Mupalya were quickly jailed at the time they were thinking of contesting for elections to go to the legislative council to voice the grievances of their people against the Batoro. The three leaders were quickly tried in a Kangaroo type of court on the eve of the London Conference of June 1962. The Bakonzo leaders wrote a letter to the central government and gave copies to the governor and the colonial secretary, complaining about the actions of the judges who passed judgment against their three leaders so that they could be left in prison while Batooro leaders went to the Conference to ask for federal status. The Bakonzo /Bamba leaders while on trial expected an acquittal since they did not have any case to answer, and were well prepared to travel to London to attend the Constitutional Conference. Instead the Batooro judges paved their way to jail.

Isaya Mukirane did not live long to see the fruits of his resistance. He fell sick with typhoid fever and died on 2nd September 1966. He was buried on Bulemba Hill in Ihandiro. A public moaning was held all over the mountain areas covering the present Kasese and Bundibugyo Districts. Isaya was moaned in the counties of Burahya, Bunyangabo, Busongora, Bakonzo, and Bwamba.

Chapter 6

Isaya Mukirane 1964

During this time, all the primary schools on the lower lands of the Rwenzori were closed. Those on the mountain areas remained open but with no teachers. The rwenzururu leadership hired teachers of all kinds, most of them were grade level, and most had not studied beyond class four. I remember one of the schools I went to at Kitabona village, the primary school had classes up to grade four and the headmaster who was also the grade four teacher, was a grade four '*graduate*'. My father did not want me to be taught in primary four by a teacher who was also a primary four graduate. He moved me to Butale School where we were 4 children in a class and the teacher there too was just a grade five graduate. Most of the schools managed and administered by the 'kingdom' leadership had ill trained personnel let alone the buildings in which they were operating. When the "king" died, in 1966, his son Charles Wesley Mumbere had barely turned 13 years and was in the kind of school which I have described above. He was not allowed to become 'king' immediately since he was under age. A team of elders surrounded him and managed the affairs of the movement until he turned 18 when he was fully coroneted as king of the Bakonzo and Bamba, in the rwenzururu movement style. Charles Wesley had special teachers who went to the Buhikira Royal Palace to tutor him. One of these teachers was Mr. Christopher Tembo Kabwemi. He was not a qualified teacher, but since all it took was one to know some Basic English and basic mathematics, he passed on some elementary teaching to the 'king'. All this was because our people did not have qualified trained manpower, a basic service that was systematically denied us by our colonizers. The generation that went to school during this period had either to be sent to the lower lands for schooling or continued in ill equipped schools without qualified teachers and just hoped for the best. I was one of those who stayed up with the rwenzururu schools. My father was one of the *'rebels'* who could not betray the movement by sending me to the lower land schools. By sending ones children to the lower land schools meant that you had become an accomplice, a hypocrite and was betraying the very movement that was fighting for your equality. These schools were managed by the Toro government and were subject to frequent attacks from the movement soldiers. By this time, they were heavily armed with spears and knives, no longer sticks and clubs. After Isaya died, the movement was divided and the people were also divided. Those who become disillusioned by the continuous fighting moved and decided to live in protected camps on the lower lands where the Uganda rifles could offer protection. They were put in camps referred to as "internal displaced people". They were locally known as "bakolikoli" meaning betrayers. The rwenzururu leaders had a general name for them as "*esyandaghangali*", which meant those who have betrayed the cause of the movement by siding with the central government. They started helping the Uganda rifles in hunting down the die-hard Rwenzururu who chose to remain on the high lands. At this time the movement had put a mechanism in place to collect graduated tax from all those who cherished and supported the cause of the movement. They now operated a government equivalent to the Toro Kingdom one. They had appointed ministers, chiefs and local leaders. The movement continued to collect graduated taxes from those faithful ones and agents who were living amongst them for spying purposes; they collected even some taxes from among the *'bakolikoli'* privately. In October of 1966 the lower land group, arrested my father for refusing to bring me to a legitimate school. He would only be released if he agreed to bring me to Kyarumba primary school. My father had no choice but to comply. That October, I came in the middle of third term to complete my grade four class. I was lucky they promoted 15 students out of a total of 16 students. Had I not been among the 15 students, I would have been forced to repeat the class. At this time my headmaster, a qualified teacher was Mr. Yosia Muhindo, famously known as Kireru. He was my English teacher and was considered at the time as the best English teacher in the whole Kasese region. He was later nominated to go for a short course in English at the University of Makerere. He was the only headmaster who was chosen by the Omukama's government to go for this prestigious course. As a result he became well known by the education authorities in the Toro district and was later transferred to head a more populated school, Karambi Primary School, which was on the lower land and controlled by the *bakolikoli* group. Mr. Muhindo became one of the best interpreters from English to Lukonzo for any foreign guest who visited the rwenzori region. This famous teacher although full of intellect, did not advance beyond head teacher at grade two level; not because he did not have school fees, but the Toro education authorities would not let him. He too was a victim of discrimination. He later retired in the 80s and became the district executive secretary, a post he held until 1985. When he left Kyarumba in 1967, another dynamic headmaster, Mr. Nyamayaro Ezra was appointed to take his place. He initiated the rebuilding of the school since it was on the brink of collapse. The Toro Government's Education Authority had neglected most schools in "disturbed" areas of the

Ruwenzori's. Kyarumba primary school was among the many schools, which did not receive any attention since the uprising of the movement. It was considered hidden in the cupboard. Mr. Nyamayaro who hails from the Kiyonga family mobilized the parents of Kyarumba School to collect money instead of depending on the Education authority to provide funding to put up a permanent block of buildings. A permanent foundation was started but got stuck and could not take off from the foundation level due to lack of extra funding from the government to reinforce what the parents provided. By 1968 the building block had not taken off. Later Ezra was transferred leaving his project unfinished. This was the first time I ever saw a head teacher of a primary school organizing a fundraising without government help. Mr. Nyamayaro set the example for building a school on self help and many schools were to follow. Kyarumba Primary School was one of the few schools that were upgraded to grade seven levels when the central government abolished the junior school system in 1966. However, grade seven did not come until 1969. The first bunch of students to attend grade seven from this school traveled seven miles to Kisinga to sit for their primary leaving exam. I was one of the first candidates to sit for grade seven at Kyarumba in 1969. Grade six graduates from this school either went to Bwera Junior School, Nsenyi junior school, or just disappeared amongst the population and started teaching in the mountain schools. Most of the manpower for the counties of Busongora and Bwamba was generated from the two junior schools we had at that time, i.e. Bwera Junior Secondary and Nsenyi Junior Secondary school. These two were established on religious foundations to cater for the two prominent religions in the area, a system that was divisive, designed by the Omukama's government to divide and rule the Bamba and Bakonzo. Most of the graduates from these two Junior Secondary Schools ended up in teachers' collages, not by choice but by design. That is Butiti Teachers' College accepted those from Nsenyi while Canon Apollo College accepted those from Bwera. Very few managed to go to Senior Secondary School. 1967 was the last year we saw Junior Secondary Schools. Government introduced legislation to abolish Junior Schools and have primary level go from primary one to primary seven whereas senior level was to go from grade nine to twelve, and high school was to go from thirteen to fourteen. With proper lobbying, this was the opportunity for the two Junior Secondary School to acquire full secondary status. As grade seven was introduced in several schools, educational materials did not reach all the schools. Many of the schools that were accorded the status of primary seven did not even have the buildings to house their grade seven students. Some hosted them under trees and others used nearby churches to accommodate this extra class. When time of examination came, the candidates for grade seven were gathered at centers where exams could be distributed. In 1968 the candidates for grade seven leaving exams from Kyarumba were asked to travel to Kisinga on foot to go and sit for the exam. At this time there was only one primary school, Kyarumba which was accorded the status of grade seven. Schools like Ngangi, Nyamusule and Mahango, which were introduced and built by the Bazarabusa initiative, could not receive primary seven status because they were under the Rwenzururu leadership and their enrolment was very low. Other schools like Kitolu, Kanyatsi, Kyondo and Nyakiyumbu suffered the same fate. Most of these schools had the building structures, but did not have the required enrolment and of course had poorly trained teachers. These however, with their meager enrolment continued to become main contributors of students to fill up the newly introduced grade seven levels. Academic performance here was not exciting mainly because the teachers were not well qualified. Again, this was a systematic ploy to keep the Bakonzo under-educated for fear of competition with the Batoro. The abolition of Junior Secondary opened a new era in the education system of the entire country, Uganda. The Rwenzori region missed an opportunity here to have at least one of their schools upgraded to secondary level during this restructure. The issue was lack of effective representation in the National Parliament. Nevertheless, this opened a new way for the Bakonzo and Bamba students to by-pass the Toro leadership to join Senior Secondary Schools in other areas of the country. The bursary allotment however was still centralized in Kabarole and only very few of the Bamba/Bakonzo students gained from the bursary scheme. The parents supported most of the students who were able to go to senior secondary schools. They had to be well-to-do parents to afford school fees. When they abolished the Junior Secondary School in 1967, Kisinga sub-county was seeing their first graduate from Makerere University, the late Dr. Baranaba Rwatooro. Interestingly enough, he went to Kisinga primary school, then Bwera Primary School and later to Kabarole Junior Secondary School. He later went to Nyakasura Secondary school before joining Makerere University. **He was the first Mukonzo to obtain a degree.** Remember his name was "Rwatoro".

When Uganda became independent in 1962, there were no graduates in Bwamba and Bukonzo/Busongora counties. The highest educated person in Bwamba was Yositasi Nzenze Bwambale. Together with Timothy Bazarabusa, they were the most highly educated personalities the Rwenzoris could offer to the central government at independence. This partly accounts for why Dr. Obote appointed Timothy Bazarabusa as Uganda's High Commissioner to United Kingdom. Very little is known of what became of Mr. Nzenze. The first Muyira from Bwera to graduate was the Late Amon Bazira. He too was product of Bwera Junior Secondary School and Nyakasura High School before he went to Makerere where he graduated in 1970. Busongora did not see their first graduate until 1980 in the name of **Jorome Mbura Muhindo**.

He went to Katiri Primary School in Kilembe and St. Mary's Kisubi before he went to Makerere University. So do you ever wonder why we did not have as many Bakonzo/Bamba boys and girls going through this Kilembe Mines School? The reason is simple. At this time, the labor force at Kilembe was dominated by Batooro and Bakiga, which meant that only their kids went to the mine schools. Mbura Muhindo is only one of the very few who went to a mine school and made it to the University.

Jerome Mbura Muhindo went to Katiri Primary school, passed his grade seven and was admitted to Kisubi Secondary School. He later joined Makerere University and graduated in 1980. He became the headmaster of Kasese Secondary after losing elections he contested first on a UPM ticket. After being defeated by Dr. Chrispus Kiyonga in the primaries, he crossed into the Democratic Party of Paul Kawanga Semogerere. He was the first student of Busongora to graduate from University. Can you imagine a whole county of Busongora receiving their first graduate twenty [20] years after independence!

By 1971 when the Infamous Gen. Idi Amin took power, Kasese District had barely 6 graduates to account for in the Rwenzori area. One wonders how many could the Omukama's kingdom account for when they had Nyakasura, St. Leos Kyegobe, Kyebambe and Mpanga, all fully government funded school spewing their products into Makerere University. I leave this to the reader to guess.

The Bakonzo/Bamba/Basongora did not see their first **female doctor until 1982 Dr. Florance Kabugho.** [RIP].

She got her degree from Makerere University Kampala. She went to Kitalikibi Primary School, Mundongo Primary school, Kyebambe Girls School, Trinity College Nabbingo and Makerere University, Kampala. She got her professional degree to practice Medicine and passed on untimely in 2001.

Education in the Rwenzoris progressed at a slow pace, as there were not many if any institutions of higher learning. The first Doctors of Philosophy [PhD] was attained in 1977 from Harvard University by Dr. Henry Edward Bwambale [RIP]. Dr. Bwambale, like many academicians from this region went through thick and thin to get this Degree. He is the first graduate to hail from Karambi Sub County. He received a Bachelor of Commerce in 1972, and later that year was able to beat the Amin regime's intelligence, as they were hunting the elite, he flew to Iraq to pursue a Masters Degree and later joined Harvard University in Boston for his Doctor of Philosophy Degree. I will discuss Dr. Bwambale's political contributions in a later chapter.

Below now find a break down of graduates by Sub County. Only 32 had graduated by 1980.

Names	Degree	Year	County
1 Dr. Rwatooro Barnabas	Ch. B, M. B	1967	Kisinga
2 Police - Apuuli Stephen	B.A.	1968	Munkunyu
3 Kitakakire Bartholomew	B.A.	1969	Kisinga
4 Bazira Amon [RIP]	B.Phil.	1970	Bwera
5 Mukiraine Joseph [RIP]	B.Sc.	1970	Kisinga
6 Kabagambe John [RIP]	B.Com	1970	Katwe
7 Kabagambe Paddy	B.Sc	1971	Karambi
8 Bwambale Henry [RIP]	B.Com.	1972	Karambi
9 Muhindo Enoch Jim Sakalombi	B.Ed	1972	Bwera
10 Bonabana Kitakakire Candida	SWASA	1972	Kisinga
11 Maate Enos	B.Com	1972	Bwera
12 Tibasaga Kitakakire Thereza	B.A. (Ed)	1973	Kisinga
13 Kighoma Eria	B.Com	1973	Munkunyu
14 Masereka Mutiba	B.A (Ed)	1973	Munkunyu
15 Muhindo Victor [RIP]	B.A	1974	Bwera
16 Abwolikiyonga Semu B	B.A	1974	Bwera
17 Kabarole Elijah	B.A	1974	Kisinga
18 Biira Hannah [RIP]	B. A (Ed)	1974	Kyarumba
19 Muhindo Mukirane Hannah	B.Sc. (Ed)	1975	Bwera
20 Byalebeka Kamabu John	B.Sc. Agric	1975	Bwera
21 Muhindo Lazaro [RIP]	B.Sc.	1975	Kisinga
22 Katanga Kitakakire John [RIP]	B.Sc. Agric	1975	Kisinga
23 Kambere Selevester	B.Com	1975	Kisinga
24 Bwambale Yostasi	B.Sc	1975	Bwera
25 Bwambale Misaki [RIP]	B.Sc. [Eng.]	1975	Bwera
26 Biira Loice	B.Sc.(Ed)	1977	Bwera
27 Mbayahi Bwambale Jethro	B. Ed	1977	Kisinga
28 Baluku Stephen	B.A.(Ed)	1976	Bwera
29 Kiyonga B. Crispus	Ch.B, M.B	1976	Bwera
30 Nduru Deo [RIP]	B.Com.	1976	Bwera
31 Kahindo David	B.Sc	1976	Bwera
32 Mbura-Muhindo Jerome	B.Sc. Ed	1980	Kilemb

Currently the number of graduates has reached beyond 500. I will discuss the reasons for this upsurge and the celebration of it in a later chapter; first, let me discuss the political era of post Isaya Mukirane. Remember, not until Amin came on the scene, we were still talking of Rwenzururu fighting for a separate kingdom even though 'kingdoms' ceased to exist in Uganda in 1967, when Uganda became a republic. On the Bwamba side of the mountain, education was as slow as was on the Bukonzo side. As I mentioned earlier along with Yokasi Bwambale Nzenze, Kawamara and Mupalia were the first graduates out of teacher training colleges with Isaya Mukirane. After them in 1961 Kibulya and Sam Katuramu followed. The next bunch came out in 1966 with the first Diploma graduate as J. Kiregheya. By 1980 the following had graduated with degrees: Dr. William Sikyeunda, Mubunga Makasi, Tom Maate, Byakutaga, Mumbere Paul and Tom Nkayarwa, the first member of the National Consultative council representative for Bundibugyo after the fall of Idi Amin in 1979.

Chapter 7

The Charles Wesley Iremangoma era: Myth or Reality?

Irema Ngoma simply means the "ruler" of the drum. In local dialect, the kingdom is referred to as the Drum, [Engoma the realm]. The Batoro referred to their king as 'Omukama' and the Bakonzo/Bamba did not want to use the same word since it was a 'Lutooro' meaning for King. The Bakonzo/Bamba came up with their own title according to the requirements of their language and tradition. To be crown king is referred to as to "erisinga" and the person who is being crown is referred to as the 'Omusinga' and the kingdom for which they are being crown is referred to as the 'Obusinga'. Therefore in this context, the Bakonzo/Bamba referred to their Kingdom as the "Obusinga Bwa

Rwenzururu" and the man in charge was referred to as the Omusinga. This can also be the substitute for "Mr". before the name. Omusinga Charles Wesley Mumbere, otherwise referred to as Irema Ngoma succeeded his father later than was expected since he was a minor at the time his father died in 1966.

Charles Mumbere was born on 14/11/1952, at 8:00 am at Ntuntu Primary School - Kitagwenda, Toro Kingdom. During that time, his father was a teacher at Ntuntu Primary School. He did not become "king' until he was 18 years. A team of elders shielded him while he grew to become of age; they run the affairs of the "obusinga". Regent Minister in the name of Yohana Mwambalaluli headed the elders. In 1966 October 19, at a colorful ceremony at Kahinda Ngoma, Kalingwe, and Charles was coroneted King of the Bakonzo/Bamba and all other tribes within the Rwenzori. Many people from the lower lands climbed the mountains to attend the ceremony. School children climbed the mountains to perform, and sing for the new King. The elders who were running the kingdom, surrendered power to Charles, and he assumed the responsibilities of the kingdom. He had grown up as Charles Kisembo, which simply meant the "gift" in the local dialect; and when he became king, the name Kisembo was overshadowed and replaced by the title "IremaNgoma". He had been called Kibanzanga 11 after his Father, which meant that the Kingdom will find him if the central government cannot give it to him. However, this changed when Charles became king, because he and the elders asserted that he was no longer waiting for the kingdom to come; it was already there and he was now the 'King'. He had been trained as a solider and he ruled the kingdom as a military king. He had not received formal education, except by special teachers who themselves were not qualified to teach. He registered to study in British Tutorial College in Nairobi taking correspondence studies in English, Maths and Geography. He used to read newspapers and magazine from overseas sent to him by Tom Stacey, the man who was close to his father and to the Bakonzo as a tribe in general.

Charles was a young and energetic king who trained and drilled with his young soldiers and changed the mode of leadership from the elderly folk's style to a youthful style with lots of young soldiers surrounding him. His training staff included two run away soldiers from the regime of Idi Amin. These were Staff Sergeant Mwagavumbi and Lt. Paul Byakatonda. Paul Byakatonda ran away from the Uganda Air force after surviving the Entebbe raid by Israel Commandoes. Idi Amin hunted all soldiers who survived the attack and called them collaborators. Paul and others took off for their dear lives and he found himself hiding in the mountains. He together with Mwagavumbi trained the king and promoted him to the rank of *"general"* at Kahindangoma school of "infantry" with a ceremony officiated by his own chief of staff *"major"* Richard Kinyamusitu. He centralized his leadership, by becoming the head of the Kingdom and the Commander-in-Chief of the army while creating the Office of the Prime Minister who was the head of the government. The Prime Minister otherwise called the *'omulerembera'* chaired cabinet meetings and oversaw the day-to-day running of the kingdom. The Omusinga Charles was the head of the Privy Council, which was seated by his appointees. This council acted as the advisory committee to the king on matters pertaining to the administration of the kingdom. He chaired the defense council as the Commander-in-Chief of the army. This council comprised of the various commanders and both the Minister of Defense and that of Internal Affairs.

When General Amin was sent by Dr. Obote to fight the Rwenzururu under Isaya Mukirane, he confronted them as militia men but when in 1969 Charles assumed leadership, General Amin found young men armed not only with spears and sticks, but with guns ranging from SMGs [submachine guns] to mortars and Rocket Propelled grenades. [RPG] The youthful Charles came with sophisticated armory and there is a mystery as to where he might have acquired these arms.

One might ask a question as to what happened to the revolution which was led by the three founders of the resistance; **Nyamutswa, Kapoli and Tibamwenda**. Indeed what happened was the suppression of human rights as these three had intended to fight for the rights of the Bayira, before they were hanged and buried in one grave at Kagando. In fact, one of them, Mr. Tibamwenda left behind a wife who was pregnant and later delivered a baby boy and named him Cyril Makoma. In all local organizations, this young boy Cyril Makoma should have succeeded his father and spear-headed the revolution, but the colonial masters at the time together with the Batoro, made sure that this revolution did not resurface. Killing the trio and burying them in one grave was meant to scare off any person related to them to ever revive the revolution. Although it was more of a traditional revolution, it was fighting for the human rights of the oppressed Bayira. Even the name Bayira from that time changed to Bakonzo; a derogatory name meaning dogs in the Ruhenda language of Tooro. Later when the white missionaries traveled over the hills of Rwenzori, they often asked which people lived on the slopes and had those beautiful gardens. But the Batooro royals could say in Kiswahili language that *"wale ni wa gonjwa"* meaning those are the sick. When the missionaries wanted to build schools and Hospitals to serve the people on the slopes of the mountain, the batoro royals replied, "Those are monkeys" [Alnaes, 1996; 294].

When Cyril Makoma grew up, he went to a catholic school and trained as a teacher and later became the headmaster of Nsenyi Junior School from 1940 –1955. In 1956, while he was headmaster of Katwe primary school, he complained to the Toro Kingdom for the execution of his father, Tibamwenda. As a response to his grievances, "the Toro Kingdom appointed him sub-county chief of Karambi" [Yona Balyaghe, Oct. 2000; 38]. The Batoro leadership sensed danger that in the person of Cyril Makoma they could have old wounds opened. They quickly promoted him to serve in the Magistrate Court office. This ended the aspiration of the *Baswagha clan* to inherit the Bakonzo/Bamba throne. Those who were on the forefront of the negotiations and pressure were frustrated and gave up the whole scheme. Almost thirty years later, a new generation of think tanks surfaced and revived the struggle for freedom and human rights. From 1954, Isaya Mukirane was involved in the Bakonzo Life History Research, and as a Muhira clan leader and a trained teacher, he was agreed upon as the leader of a revolution, which would revive the grievances, aired by the Bakonzo traditional leaders; three of whom had been hanged thirty years earlier. The Baswagha and Basu clan leaders blessed the crowning of Isaya, a Muhira by clan, because among those who should have been crowned as clan leaders were Cyril Makoma, a Musu by clan, and Basikania, son of Mukeri. These two refused to be crowned together with Isaya because they feared to die like Nyamutswa, Kapoli and Tibamwenda. It is from this brave Isaya, that we get the child Charles Kisembo Mumbere who later became 'king' with a revolutionary vision.

In 1969 the former regent Mr. Mwambala died and a certain Bawalana came on the scene. He planned to stage a palace coup by trying to sideline Charles, take over the home of Isaya, had a relationship with Isaya's wife and introduced a kind of religious cult, which was not common to what Charles had grown to know. This scheme by Bawalana caused a lull in the fighting, there was some relative peace until Charles stood his ground in 1970 and threw Bawalana out of the palace. As mentioned earlier, he continued to receive rigorous military training by Amin's deserters in 1976 after the Entebbe raid by the Israel commandoes who had come to rescue their hostages.

Only insiders and not commoners knew the myth surrounding the kingdom. To date the mythology still reigns around the kingdom, the myth has lived among the people, and this same myth has made them united around the kingdom for years. After King Charles drove Bawalana away from the palace, he devised a method of ruling which became a mystery to everyone. He became both a king and a military leader. It was very difficult to find him in one place as well; he tended to live in several palaces. There was no specific headquarters, although the name Buhikira Royal Palace has often been floated. Even in Harrisburg USA we had a Buhikira Royal palace. It was extremely hard for any common person to know how the "kingdom" operated. They had a mechanism of collecting taxes but the accountability of those taxes was never known to many.

There was enormous fear of the movement. Whenever soldiers of the king were sighted in any neigbourhood, people often fled because either they feared to pay the tax or to be asked to carry food for the establishment. The Bakonzo have seen this kingdom as a tool to highlight their grievances notably neglect and abuse of human rights by the then Toro Kingdom to the central Ugandan government. Political leaders have manipulated the people and used this myth of the revolution to gain votes from the public, because what comes from the mouth of the throne is generally respected by the people of the districts of Bundibugyo and Kasese. Indeed the mythology around this kingdom has brought dignity to a people who were least known in the country.

Mighty leaders like Amin and Obote who had trained armies were not able to penetrate through their own trained intelligence into the obusinga kingdom. A few selected individuals around the King himself only knew the mechanism through which the kingdom was run. Researchers have written papers about this movement, but nobody has been able to come face to face with where the establishment was being governed from. During the negotiations to bring the rebellion to a stop, the Uganda People's Congress government used Amon Bazira, MP and Amos Kambere MP to broker a peace deal. Amon Bazira used to come with huge amounts of money to give to the kingdom so that they stop collecting taxes from civilian population. We were however never allowed to come close to where the central governance was located. Irema Ngoma's father used to hide in what was called the furthest private cave. But for Charles, nobody knows if he even had a private cave or if the mountain from which we all derived our livelihood was his private cave. The snow caped mountain of the moon is significant in the lives of all the Banyarwenzururu for being home to the furtherest private caves, and for providing way of escape from many dangers that arise from either countries, Uganda on one side and Congo on the other. The mountain shall remain a cherished institution to the people of the Rwenzori region.

Chapter 8

"Idi Amin (also known as Idi Amin Dada) was the naughty, ruthless dictator of the African nation of Uganda during the 1970s. He started out as a soldier in the British colonial army in 1946 and became one of its first Ugandan commissioned officers. Amin rose through the ranks and was eventually made the army's chief of staff under Uganda's first president, Milton Obote. In 1971 Amin overthrew Obote and seized power."

It was 2:00 am pacific time, August 16th 2003 on the Pacific Coast of North America. I was wide awake watching late night television. The Canadian broadcasting Corporation [CBC] announces the death of a renowned world dictator. The news hit headlines. "Idi Amin Dada was dead after one month in coma in a Saudi Arabian Hospital." The Canadian Broadcasting Corporation newscaster read; "He called himself His Excellency Dr. Idi Amin Dada, V.C. DSO, M.C, King of Scotland, Life President of Uganda and Conqueror of The British Empire."[cbctv 2003] What the Western media did not know was that Amin was Al-Hajji, he was also Chancellor of Makerere University and in 1975 he was the Chairman of Organization of African Unity. All those titles used to come after his name especially when the local news were being read on Uganda radio and television,

Amin was a world dictator, no doubt about that and sometimes referred to as the buffoon of Africa and a cannibal; he was responsible for the death of thousands of people in Uganda including the Arch Bishop of Uganda's Anglican Church. He is believed to have murdered one of his several wives, but to some Ugandans he was a *"savior and a Pan Africanist."* If you follow his speeches and ideology, you will realize that Amin lacked coherence in his policies though they were all geared at a better Uganda in a united African. He just did not know how to articulate his ideas. He was not educated enough to even reason politically let alone intellectually. **He just did not know how to rule.** As he took power, he inherited written programs left behind by Milton Obote and since he was semi illiterate, he had quite a hard time filling up the puzzle and fitting into Obote's wide shoes. He missed his point when he turned against his enemies with an iron feast and his agents brutally killed and maimed many. Amin took power in Uganda on January 25, 1971. At that time the Bakonzo and Bamba had almost exhausted all avenues with the government of Milton Obote to secure peace and respect for human rights in their area. They had resorted to wanton fighting even among themselves notwithstanding their target, to secure for themselves a United Kingdom separate from that of the Batooro. Since Kingdoms had ceased to exist by 1967, the Bakonzo/Bamba had shifted course and were now demanding for a separate district. To them the whole idea was to move away from the administration of the Batooro. As soon as Idi Amin ceased power by the barrel of the gun, he declared a cease fire with the Rwenzururu, because he had been the army commander and knew the trouble he would face as president if he did not declare cease fire with King Charles Kisembo Iremangoma.

Irema Ngoma, King of the Banyarwenzururu however, ignored Amin's offer of the cease fire and went on burning Bakonzo huts and rolling stones whenever Amin's forces came to the mountain areas. The border area between Kasese and Kabarole and between Bwamba and Kabarole on the other side of the mountain became hostile areas and almost a no-go zone. The youthful King Irema Ngoma was often seen on the frontline with his soldiers fighting anyone who opposed the kingdom and anyone who refused to pay the Rwenzururu tax. The Rwenzururu fighters were planning to take the fighting all the way to Muzizi River in Kabarole district, a river they believed was the border of the Kingdom before Kasagama took it over and handed it over to the Batoro.

The population in both Kasese and Bundibughyo were generally thrilled to see Obote go and Amin take over. As there were jubilations in the whole country celebrating the departure of Milton Obote, there were skepticism among the Rwenzururu leadership about the arrival of Amin, a man who in 1968 and 1969 had presided over the burning and destruction of property belonging to Banyarwenzururu in the Rwenzori region. The council of elders who surrounded the Irema Ngoma as advisers did not trust him even though he was now President of the Republic of Uganda. Amin had been both field commander and at the same time the Army Chief of Staff. So most of the decisions Obote took were based on the advices Amin gave him. He partly was to blame for failure to bring peace in the region. While members of the Democratic Party in Parliament were calling for the Bakonzo to be wiped out so that the area could be declared into a National Park, Amin was in full gear commanding his National troops to kill, rape and maim innocent civilians. They did these horrible acts of gross human rights violation because the Bakonzo either failed or refused to show them the way that lead to the Irema Ngoma's palace. Some members of the Democratic Party in Parliament even stooped so low as to call for the castration of the Bakonzo tribe so that they stop producing more children. In spite of all these, the Bakonzo and Bamba did not resent the Democratic Party, as I discussed in previous chapters.

Amin, during his takeover speech declared, "I am not a politician, I am a professional solider" [Uganda Argus Jan/26, 1971]. But when you look at the way he handled the Banyarwenzururu matters, it was typical political tactics. In 1972 while people were still celebrating his rise to power, some young Bakonzo boys and men decided that in order for them to be noticed and present their demands in person, they will 'walk' to state house Entebbe to officially thank him for removing Obote who had refused to separate them from the Batooro. They would then demand that he does the noblest of thing; grant them separation. Volunteers were recruited and quite a sizable number of people made the trek to the State House Entebbe, a journey of almost 300 kilometers. They walked through Fort Portal, Mubende, Mityana, Kampala and then Entebbe. Amin received them and later gave them a plane back to Kasese. As a professional soldier, he met with this delegation dressed in military fatigue and told the youth that he would be meeting with the elders of both Kasese and Bwamba.

A delegation chaired by Mr. Daudi Muhindo a.k.a Isebira prepared to meet with Amin to present a memorandum representing all the Banyarwenzururu. Among the delegation were Mr. Ezironi Bitaaba and Hajji Muhamoud Baluku. The Irema Ngoma Privy Council did not approve this delegation and did not contribute any suggestions to ideas and points that were put in the memorandum. Nevertheless, Daudi Muhindo and his team went a head and prepared to meet with Amin and push for a separate district for the Banyarwenzururu.

When Idi Amin took power, most Ugandans were worried about what Obote had pronounced at Lugogo in 1969, at the Uganda

Peoples Congress annual delegates conference. He had announced the "Common Man's Charter". The majority of Ugandans did not understand what would come out of this so-called Common Man's Charter, a policy statement that would have steered the country towards socialist progressive programs.

Amin used this as one of the reasons why he took over government. But the more painful question has remained: was this Amin's idea to take power? Throughout his leadership in the late 1960s, Dr. Apolo Milton Obote was consolidating his grip on power and introducing democratic legislation that was to shake the colonial interests. Although Obote was not a Castrol or a Kaddafi, his common man's charter I mentioned earlier and the nationalization of almost 80 British companies were not welcomed in by Her Majesty's government. Obote was on the point of changing not only the constitution but the whole political system when the coup occurred. Uganda was a vital source of raw materials and for this reason was not about to be permitted to determine its own political development at the expense of the entrenched colonial interest. Therefore plans were put in place by Britain, Israel, and America to remedy the growing situation. As they planned to remove Dr. Obote from power, they had to quickly find a possible successor who would serve their best interest. Idi Amin became that choice. The British knew him since he served as a non commissioned officer in the British colonial regiment as well as with the British as they were suppressing the rebellion in Mau Mau area of Kenya. Amin as he was aided to take power, he appointed a cabinet of intellectuals who were opposed to the Uganda Peoples Congress Party. He brought in people like Edward Rugumayo, Abu Mayanja, Luimbazi Zake, Wanume Kibedi, Charles Ondonga, Henry Kyemba and others but none from the ranks of the Bakonzo and Bamba. This was partly because he could not find an "intellectual" who was ministerial material. The Bakonzo had just had their sixth graduate from Makerere University since independence.

At the time Amin took over power, Uganda had four administrative regions, thus Northern, Western, Eastern and Buganda regions. There were 18 districts in total. When the Bakonzo elders presented their memorandum, it had so many demands, but the most notable ones were the demand for a separate district, the establishment of secondary schools and a district hospital. Since independence there were no secondary schools in Kasese and Bundibugyo and there was no hospital in Kasese. This perhaps explains why at his take over, there were barely six men who had graduated from University in the whole district.

Although Amin, at his inauguration as President, had proclaimed that he was a professional solider and not a politician, the Bakonzo case put him to test and was forced to make a political decision that affected the entire country. He made a determination that if he answered the demands of the Bakonzo alone he would have the Batooro jumping up in arms to resist the solved equation. Indeed he would become unpopular among the Batooro because he would have pleased their traditional enemies. As well, he would be setting up a bad precedent by opening up a window where any disagreement among any tribe in Uganda to call for separation would ensue, which means he would have a handful of grievances coming from the diverse tribes of the entire country.

So he took of the military hat and put on the "political" one and made a political decision. He decided that in order to solve the burning problems of the Bakonzo and Bamba he was not to give them the schools or hospitals, but was to allow them to be governed as separate districts. Instead of announcing that the Bakonzo and Bamba were given separate districts from Toro, Amin announced that every District in Uganda would be divided into two for easy administration and that Toro would be divided into three. He started with Ankole which now gave birth to East Ankole and West Ankole. He divided Acholi District to become North Acholi and south Acholi districts, and for Toro, he divided it to become Rwenzori District and Semuliki districts. One will notice that Most of the Districts in Uganda kept their originals names save for the additions of either East or West or North and South. For the Bakonzo, the name Toro had to be eliminated from their vocabulary and that brought sense of satisfaction and comfort among the Bakonzo and Bamba who praised Amin as "the

Man" finally at last. Towards the end of 1973 the District of Rwenzori was born and Maja Alur became the first district commissioner.

Amazingly professional solider, was turned into a Politician who tried to solve the question of the Banyarwenzuru. However this did not please the "Irema Ngoma privy council" which denounced the announcement as a mere fuss. They argued that Amin did not actually give them their district. First they argued that the borders were not defined and that much of their land remained in Toro [now Kabarole]. They also argued that the district was empty without indigenous people working in it. "It was like giving you a match box without matches", said one of the privy councilors. At this point the war would rage on and Irema Ngoma would continue to fight until his people realized and assumed full leadership of their district. In 1973, even when the district had been granted, some Bakonzo scholars from Makerere University decided that they would try to convince the leadership of the Rwenzururu Kingdom to abandon fighting, which had caused untold suffering among their people. One among these scholars was Mr. Kireru who made several efforts to try to meet with the Irema Ngoma's Privy council to see if he could discuss the idea of abandoning hostilities and concentrating efforts to fighting by the book and by the pen. Kireru as one of the leaders of Rwenzori Students' Association, made several attempts to climb the mountains in an effort to seek audience with the King himself. He was being sent by the Daudi Muhindo's committee to arrange a meeting with the Privy Council. At this point it was believed that the Privy Council was expecting to meet Daudi Muhindo and was prepared to arrest him for going a head to meet with Amin without consulting them.

Mr. Kereru

Instead they saw the young Kireru coming uphill. On that fateful occasion while he was climbing the mountains in Kyanzuki, Kilembe sub county, he was arrested and later that day killed by the very people he thought would lead him to the King. He was mourned greatly by the local people, the school children and the students at the university. This happened in 1973 after Amin had announced the subdivisions of districts and Bakonzo and Bamba had benefited from this announcement of the new districts. Irema Ngoma continued to resist the rule of Idi Amin because his privy council contended that the central government had given us the district without resources and the Bakonzo would not even get jobs. The core issue here was not the district, but was lack of education and educational institutions, hospitals, and the infrastructure. The king himself lacked complete education. These services had to be in place for anyone to assume that development had come to an area. When confronted with the question of killing people even the educated few, Irema Ngoma has always defended his soldiers' actions that they did not intend to harm indigenous people, but that during any struggle, there is always loss of life and he has since apologized for such unintentional losses of human life and property. Mr. Kireru's death scared off scholars from making further attempts to persuade the Irema Ngoma to abandon fight and causing untold suffering to the people he claimed were his subjects. However as the myth surrounding the Kingdom grew, so support for the Rwenzururu movement continued to grow as well.

Chapter 9

THE GATE WAY TO EDUCATION – THE THIRD CLASS TRAIN VOYAGE

As the Rwenzururu rebellion was raging on, the parents in Kasese and Bundibugyo did not relent on education. They did not care whether Fort Portal did not admit their children in the government and private schools that were already established. There was one gateway through which some daring parents and their children capitalized on. This was the Railway that joined Kampala city to Kasese. The train at that time was the only gateway to the capital city, Kampala where several day schools and private schools became the main resource for the Bakonzo and Bamba to educate their children. A few of such schools were Old Kampala Senior Secondary School, His Highness the Aga Khan Secondary school, Kololo Senior Secondary School, Mengo Secondary school, Kitante High school and Kibuli Moslem High school. The private schools included Bashir High school and Muhmoud High school. The graduates of these schools formed the elite class in Rwenzori and Bwamba. The students who went to these schools passed through untold hardships in order to acquire education. Between 1970 and 1974 the education system left behind by the UPC regime was still functioning and the bursary structure was still working. Because bursaries were sent to schools from each district, it was mandatory that some money were sent to government schools whether they were day schools or boarding schools. The amount was allotted according to students per district. Therefore the kids who were in the Kampala schools mostly came from Kasese and not Toro. This means when it came to giving out bursaries to students who came from Toro and attended schools such as Old Kampala Secondary School, the majority happened to be coming from the Bakonzo land. This is the only way we benefited from the bursary scheme. Each student was allocated two hundred Uganda shillings and fees were in most cases one hundred and forty shillings for day schools. Each student would then be invited to the headmaster's office to be told that they received a bursary of 200/- which covered the school fees. The student had a choice to withdraw the 60/- or save it for next term if they were unsure whether they would receive more assistance. In most cases the students chose to withdraw the balance as this was the only pocket money most Bakonzo students would survive on for the entire three months of school term. Some of these students just left their home in Bukonzo with a bag of about 40 kilograms of cassava flour [kaunga], about 10 kilograms of beans and about 5 kilograms of dry ground nuts that would last them three months. They would arrive in Kampala where they knew nobody, and find rented accommodation or some home stay of some sort. For those who attended Kyambogo College school, they used to stay in boys quarters of teachers houses. The same applied to those who attended Mengo Secondary School. Those who went to Old Kampala and Aga Khan School did not have this privilege because these were purely Indians schools. It was difficult to find accommodation from teachers' quarters, therefore African students, who were mainly from Kasese ganged together and lived in a suburb called Nakulabye while others lived in Kasubu. These were central places which served Old Kampala, Mengo and Aga Khan. Transportation to Kampala was cheap. Students paid concession tickets at 2.75/- in the third class. The full fare in third class was 5.25/-. The parents who accompanied their first time students to Kampala could not afford to travel in second or first class. So they sat with their children in the third class. The journey took exactly 12 hours and it was always over night. Students left Kasese at 6:00pm and arrived in Kampala either at about 6:00am. During this time, the train system was efficient and enabled parents to educate their children. One such student who benefited from this train system is the second Bishop of Rwenzori diocese the Rt. Rev. Jackson Nzerebende, a graduate of H.H.The Aga Khan School [later known as Kampala High School]. Mr. Jackson went to Bukuku Theological College after high school and was ordained a priest and served in the newly created diocese of South Rwenzori. He later joined the University of Mokono to graduate with a degree in Theology; he was later elected the second Bishop of South Rwenzori diocese, the creation of which I will discuss in a later chapter. There are other persons who benefited from the gateway. The first indigenous person to occupy the office of District Treasurer, Mr. Leo Bwambale was a graduate of Mahmud High School, a private school that admitted students from Kasese who did not find places in the Kampala school. One of the young people, who walked from Kasese to Entebbe to see Idi Amin, had just dropped out of Bashir High School near Wandengeya in Kampala. His name was Matayo. After having a meeting with Idi Amin, he was appointed to work in the Queen Elizabeth Park as a game ranger. Some of the girls who did not have money to travel to Kampala and probably did not pass very well to be officially admitted just jumped on the train to go and loiter in Kampala until they found a school that would take them. It did not matter whether they got a private school or any day government school; what mattered here was that they needed post primary education. The schools were not available in their district; they had to look for them in the capital city which did not discriminate. In 1972 when Amin expelled the Asians, the three schools which were predominantly Indians schools, i.e. Kololo High School, Aga Khan Secondary School, and Old Kampala Secondary School became depopulated. The most affected one was the Aga Khan. The ministry of education had to move some streams from Old Kampala and Kololo to come and fill up classes at the Aga Khan, because they needed to keep all the schools running. A few boys from Kasese who attended Old Kampala were moved to Aga Khan. During the following year, 1973, admissions were more flexible so that more Africans were admitted into these Kampala schools. This encouraged more of the

Kasese boys and girls to just travel to Kampala to find schools. For some who did not get enough fees to find a school in Kampala, or simply dropped out after a year or two in senior, they joined the Amin army as soldiers. Others joined the police after senior four if they could not go to higher school certificate. Because there was that bond of students from Kasese, those who joined the army would frequently visit their friends who were still going to school. Most of the students who came from Kasese did not bring enough food rations to last them the entire three months. Therefore their friends who had joined the army came to their rescue by bringing them some of the army ration. There were so many ways these boys survived in the capital city, but all in all they acquired some level of education. The Rwenzori boys and girls will never forget the train that transported them to Kampala and the support they received from each other as they lived far away from home to secure an education. As we received the district, graduates from these Kampala schools eventually came to work in Kasese. Mr. Leo Bwambale, a graduate of Mahmud secondary school became the first Mukonzo district treasure and with him came many boys to work as clerks and administrative assistants. Maja Alur was the first district commissioner appointed by Idi Amin to head the district. He was a native of West Nile district. He encouraged as many qualified indigenous boys to apply for jobs at the district level.

Chapter 10

FROM THE NATIONAL TEACHERS UNIVERSITY TO NATIONAL ASSEMBLY OF UGANDA [1978 -1984]

March 1978 I graduated as high school teacher and was posted to teach in Kigezi High School situated in the district of Kabale. I taught senior two and three. While at Kigezi High School, I did some statistics of students leaving this particular school to be admitted to Makerere University. In that year [1978] we had 68 boys and girls who sat for their Higher School Certificate Examination. Demographically, out of the 68 students, 60 were natives of Kigezi district; therefore they were Bakiga by tribe. We had one from Lango, one from Kasese, one from Kabarole, two from Buganda, and three from Mbarara district. Out of the 68 students, we had 60 students who passed very well and were eligible to be admitted to the University. Out of the 60, 52 were Bakiga coming from Kigezi district. These data clearly suggested me that because the school was locally situated in Kigezi, the majority of the students who go to that school are from the local areas and therefore the majority to be admitted to the University will come from that local district. When I looked at other schools around the same district, they had similar statistics. So in one year, because we had three secondary schools in one district all offering high school certificate, there was at least an average of 50 students coming from each school going to the University. This meant that in one year there were at least 150 students coming from one district plus those students who opted to go to other schools in Uganda. When you look at the total number of students from Kabale, the Bakiga being admitted to Makerere University, the number jumped to at least 200 because 50 catered for students who were in schools like Ntare, Budo, Gayaza, Namiliango, and Nyakasura who all came from Kigezi district as their home. Because Kasese did not have a secondary school at the time, we were only able to send about five students to Makerere compared to 200 from a similar nearby district: realistically where is the equality and justice here? Who do we blame for this imbalance? The answer is in lack of schools. I discussed this situation with my mentor Mr. Enoch Muhindo who was at the time lecturing at Kyambogo University College where I had just graduated. He agreed with me as I shared the statistics with him because he had been a teacher at Kigezi High School before he went to Kyambogo. We both agreed that the answer lied within us. We had to open schools ourselves and stop blaming the Toro Kingdom, which was long gone. We would be shedding crocodile tears if we continued to place the blame on the Batoro.

In 1979 the war to overthrow the dictator *"omunyoro Dada"* was raging on and we prayed hard for its success. When the city of Mbarara fell to the fighting forces that were composed of Tanzanian soldiers and the Ugandan exiles, there were celebrations in Kabale as we saw Amin's soldiers fleeing for their lives. Brig. David Oyite Ojok was in charge of the Masaka axis heading for the capital Kampala while Yoweri Museveni and Rurangaranga were in charge of the western axis responsible to see that there was no mayhem in the west as Amin's soldiers were fleeing. On April 11, 1979 we heard the announcement on radio Uganda, the voice was that of David Oyite Ojok announcing that Kampala city had fallen and that Amin had fled. A UNLF – Uganda National Liberation Front was formed and Yosufu Lule was declared president as elected by exiles during the Moshi conference. Yoweri Museveni was defense minister in that government, David Oyite Ojok was chief of staff and Major Edward

Rurangaranga was deputy minister of Local government. As the UNLF government's army the UNLA was sweeping all cities of the remnants of Amin's notorious boys, party leaders were sending their members to begin introducing their party policies to schools and communities in preparation for the promised elections. At Kigezi High School we were visited by two middle aged individuals who introduced themselves as Ruhakana-Rugunda and Amama-Mbabazi respectively. They requested to speak to students in the main hall, and we allowed them. Later they spoke to the staff and we fired them with questions. These two individuals were at one time UPC youth wingers before Amin over threw their government in 1971. They came back from exile as members of a new party they called UPM – Uganda Patriotic Movement. Within a couple of months, 68 days to be precise the UNLF government had fallen and Prof. Yosufu Lule had been deposed and replaced by former UPC attorney general Mr. Godfrey Lukongwa Binaisa QC.

After Rugunda and Amama Mbabazi had left our school, we realized that the entire student body did not buy into their philosophy. We opened up a UPC branch at the school and we elected an executive committee of which I was elected secretary for this branch. The UPM did not have enough members to open a branch at the school. A month after we established the UPC branch I was visited by two individuals from Kasese district with a letter from Amon Bazira.

Amon Bazira was the Director General of Intelligence in Lule's government and later in Binaisa's government. President Yusufu Lule appointed him on recommendation of the National Consultative Council of which Edward Rugumayo was the chairman. Amon

Bazira was a native of Bwera Sub County and was the first graduate to come from Bwera in 1970. During Amin's time, he was doing private business as an advertising consultant on Kampala road opposite the general post office. He was also doing underground intelligence work for the UPC and sending private massages to Tanzania. He successfully did this without being detected by Amin's killer squad using his advertising business as the cover. In 1978 around about February, Amin's intelligence zeroed up on him and he was finally netted and locked up in Naguru military unit under the notorious Ali Towili. He was going to be killed but was saved by the king of Rwanda, King Kigeri, a friend of Amin Dada. The King petitioned Amin by pleading for Bazira's release. Kigeri told Amin that the enemies of the Bakonzo were framing Bazira. Kigeri gave the example of how Bazarabusa was killed in fake motor accident, a plot believed to have been organized by the enemies of the Bakonzo/Basongoro. Amin listen and believed the King and Amon Bazira was released. As he left Naguru police torture chambers, he ran to Kasese and lived in hiding in Bwera among his Basongora tribe until Amin was overthrown. During all this time, he was rarely seen in his native land, probably as a cover so that he is not pointed out to the bad elements. He quickly moved into Kampala as Oyite Ojok announced the fall of the regime.

In 1979 the Rwenzururu fighters under 'king' Charles Irema Ngoma seized the city of Kasese and chased away all the non-bakonzo civil and public servants. They staged their front line on river Rwimi and killed many Batoro who were attempting to cross over to Kasese. The Rwenzururu soldiers acquired many arms from the fleeing soldiers. Kasese district was the gateway and escape route for the Amin soldiers who ended up in the Congo, [Zaire at that time]. One of the conditions to allow them safe escape was the surrender of their arms to the Rwenzururu soldiers. On the central government side, we had the TPDF – Tanzanian Peoples' Defense Forces taking care of the peace in the area. As soon as they realized that the Bakonzo were fighting amongst themselves, they ignored them because for them all they were after were the fleeing Amin's soldiers. The TPDF was not ready to medal into internal political issue. This helped Charles

Kisembo Iremangom organize his troops and seized control over many areas of the district. Local people as well as the Rwenzururu army had disarmed most of the fleeing soldiers. Rwenzururu was transformed from a rag tag arm of spears and clubs to a rebel army with sub machine guns and mortars.

Mr. Edward Rugumayo was the chairman of the NCC. Kasese had a representative in the NCC. His name was Dr. Henry Bwambale. Mr. Rugumayo summoned a meeting comprised of the Member of the NCC, Dr. Bwambale, and the Army Chief of Staff, Maj. General David Oyite Ojok plus the Director General of Intelligence Mr. Amon Bazira. They met to see how they could resolve the conflict that was brewing up by the boarder of Kasese and Kabarole districts, and they wanted to recapture Kasese back from the Irema Ngoma rebel army. Rugumayo is a native of Kabarole while Bazira and Bwambale were natives of Kasese. Oyite Ojok was the neutral figure in this meeting at the same time he commanded the army that would be responsible for quelling the rebellion. There was civil unrest in Kasese and Kabarole; the administrative infrastructure had broken down, and the government had a duty to restore peace between the warring parties. After this meeting, Rugumayo as Chairman of NCC [National Consultative Council], ordered David Oyite Ojok, Amon Bazira and the member of NCC Mr. Bwambale to visit the district and see if they could talk to the Rwenzururu leadership to stop the insurgencies. A military solution was not the answer since this had been tried before and had miserably failed.

The country was preparing for an election the following year, 1980. These people were charged with a responsibility of stabilizing the region so that a peaceful election could be conducted. You would note here that David Oyite Ojok was a member of Uganda Peoples' Congress, and so was Amon Bazira. Dr. Henry was a member of the Democratic Party. So we had two people here both coming from Bwera each with different political agenda; to try to stop the Rwenzuru from fighting the Batoro. Amon Bazira had made several contacts with Irema Ngoma during the time he was hiding from Amin after he left Naguru. So at least he had a starting point. He met the Rwenzururu leaders together with Oyite Ojok. Since they were both in the business of taking care of national security, they chose to meet the Rwenzururu leaders at their front line. They excluded Dr. Henry Bwambale because he was a civilian. They used their military muscle to convince and lure the Rwenzururu fighters into a meeting at Hima cement factory. At this meeting they agreed with the fighters to declare and honor a cease-fire. Under the conditions of a cease-fire, Amon Bazira promised to negotiate with the government to allow Rwenzururu leaders to appoint chiefs in Kasese District, as well as getting an indigenous Mukonzo to be head of the district as District Commissioner. If this deal went through, he was to be the first District Commissioner to come from Kasese district since independence. He had to be a person acceptable to the Irema Ngoma Privy Council as well as having the qualification acceptable to the public service commission. Amon Bazira quickly suggested the name of Mr. Blasio Maate, Headmaster of Bwera Primary School and was acceptable to the Rwenzururu negotiators. However, he was not acceptable to the public service commission, because he was not qualified. He was a grade three teacher only acceptable by the teaching service commission, and not the public service commission. Nevertheless he was a reputable personality among the Bakonzo. He had been jailed during the Omukama of Toro upraising and had been exiled into a jail in Northern Uganda, because he was with Isaya Mukirane in the initial revolt. This was the only name that would resonate well among the Bakonzo tribes' men as well as the Rwenzururu leadership.

Mr. Amon Bazira had to use his political skill to convince the ministry of public service to waive the conditions and allow Mr. Maate to be appointed District Commissioner if this was a recipe to quell a rebellion. It was an uphill task, but worth the gamble because this was better than the shedding of blood that was still raging on between the Batooro and the Bakonzo. Bazira undertook this gamble by himself leaving Dr. Bwambale Henry out of the picture. This would be a heavy political potato for Amon Bazira as he knew at the back of his mind that a district commissioner would be very important during the political nominations.

In 1979 Mr. Bulasio Maate became the first Mukonzo to occupy the office of District Commissioner. He replaced Edward Sempebwa who had been appointed by the public service commission during the late days of Idi Amin.

The Irema Ngoma council was allowed to appoint two Saza or County chiefs and Mr. Kamabu Yonasani occupied the office at Kisinga county headquarters while Mr. Paul Rwibende occupied the office at Rukoki county headquarters. Both men were unqualified for these offices, but this was necessary in order to stop the bloodshed that was raging on along the Rwimi River.

There was peace in Kasese under Blasio Maate. The Rwenzururu leadership observed the cease fire. Amon Bazira had convinced them to stop collecting taxes from the population. He had opted to bringing them hard cash from the government to sustain the leadership with a core of a few soldiers who stayed with the King. Majority of the soldiers were appointed as local askaris at the county and sub county headquarters as those of the central government had fled during the time Rwenzururu was in control of the townships. Bazira used his special branch and intelligence account to draw heavy sums of money to give to the Rwenzururu leaders. This helped Bazira build his confidence and trust among the local leaders as well as the Privy Council. There was no single person other than Bazira who had the leverage to marshal huge amounts of shillings to give to the Rwenzururu leadership. They had stopped collecting money from civilians. It would take a heavy weight with government connections to get the huge amounts for money and to be able to account for it in a security language. The president's office was fully supportive of every move that was taken. Minister Chris Rwakasisi and Amon Bazira were both in the business of National security and therefore they knew how to maneuver and get away with huge sums with minimum if not private accountability. Here people's lives were at stake therefore it did not matter how much money was drawn from the security pocket as long as war would stop and people would live in harmony with each other.

The following year was a year of campaigns. Mr. Amon Bazira resigned his job as director general of intelligence because he saw an opportunity to serve his district and would use the Rwenzururu leaders to run his campaign since he had established a good relationship with them and convinced them that Uganda Peoples Congress had the capacity to win the elections. Dr. Obote had just returned from exile on May 27 1980 and was given a reception that befitted a head of state; a strong message to the electorate that he would win the forth coming elections. At this time Godfrey Lukongwa Binaisa had been removed from power as president after 9 months and was replaced by a more hardliner UPC die-hard, Mr. Paul Muwanga. Yoweri Museveni was reduced to less important ministry of Regional cooperation and Vice Chairman to Paul Muwanga. It is from this point of view that Bazira started looking for individuals who would work with him to see Uganda Peoples Congress win seats in Kasese. He sent a letter to me in Kabale inviting me to meet with him in Kasese to discuss the possibility of standing for the UPC party.

I was in the middle of giving exams at the end of 1979 and I was due to travel to Kampala to mark the O'level exams. Instead I traveled to Kasese, and met with Amon Bazira who briefed me about the strategy of using the Rwenzururu leaders to run the UPC campaign. This was an opportunity for me to introduce my Education agenda to the people first and then to the government. I accepted his request, returned to Kabale to wind up the school year, resigned my teaching position and joined Bazira in the bid to see UPC win seats in Kasese, so that we can talk about education, unemployment, indigenous people getting jobs, and peace in our district. Literacy, job creation and peace were to be my campaign themes.

Bazira had held a few meetings with the Rwenzururu leadership and had suggested to the 'king' Irema Ngoma that for them to have a voice in the government, the entire movement had to support the Uganda Peoples' Congress. Bazira had explained to the leadership why he thought UPC would win the election. He had explained that Obote had returned from Tanzania, where the Ugandan rebels came with TPDF to remove Idi Amin. He had explained that David Oyite Ojok who was the chief of staff was from Obote's tribe and played a major role in removing Amin and bringing Obote home. He also mentioned that Paul Muwanga who was now the chairman of the military commission was a staunch UPC supporter and several cabinet ministers at the time were mostly from Uganda Peoples' Congress party. It was therefore common knowledge that if UPC won the elections, a district had to have UPC members of parliament in order to have a voice in the Government. This was the only way the Rwenzururu grievances would be heard if they returned UPC members to parliament. The Irema Ngoma Privy council agreed and were ready to listen to directions from Amon Bazira as to how they would help promote the UPC party in a predominantly DP area. During prior elections in 1961 and 1962 Toro district had voted for the Democratic Party and had remained so during the 1980 elections. Kasese and Bundibugyo were part of Toro and even though they had separated by way of districts, they still carried the sentiments of the Democratic Party. Bazira had to break this trend in order to be returned as UPC. One of the suggestions he gave to the King was for the Privy Council to announce that the people will support only one party. Having members of the Privy Council attend public rallies that were organized by the Uganda Peoples' Congress party would reinforce this declaration. They could have chosen to say no, but they believed in what Bazira told them. In actual sense, the UPC first had to convince the Rwenzururu movement leaders before they went after the general population. Bazira already knew his own people's history by the way they voted in the past. So all he wanted was to have a strong bargain with the movement while isolating the democratic party of Dr. Henry Bwambale. The Rwenzururu movement relented because they knew that through Bazira they would have direct access to the top leadership should the UPC win the elections. They had seen this evidently when he facilitated them to meet with the Chief of Staff and later with President Godfrey Binaisa. This was the first time Rwenzururu leaders had ever had direct talks with the President of Uganda. Bazira had something to offer unlike Dr. Bwambale, a member of the Democratic Party who sat in the National Consultative Council; the defacto parliament at the time when the war was raging on at the Kasese and Toro border. Bazira had used his military intelligence cap to build confidence among the Rwenzururu, unlike Bwambale, a civilian with more of an academic background. He depended on the historic voting of the people and assumed that the Democratic Party would ride high as it had always done in the past. He was wrong as he was already out maneuvered by the shrewd Bazira.

Chapter 11

THE 1980 ELECTION

Dr. Apollo Milton Obote returned from exile in Tanzania on May 27th 1980. He landed in Mbarara airport and was transported in a huge motorcade to Bushenyi as he was accorded presidential reception. I traveled from Kabale to attend this mammoth rally. From here I went to Kasese and met with Amon Bazira. We moved to Kyarumba, my hometown centre with him to assess the support UPC had among the people. As soon as we arrived at the trading centre, a small crowd of people assembled; among them were Mr. Christopher Tembo and Banginalia John. Both of these gentle men had been with Irema Ngoma in the mountains as a teacher and member of Privy Council respectively.

Bazira and I addressed them briefly and informed them that there was need for them to organize a sub county UPC committee, which would be responsible to nominate me when time comes. We moved on to Kisinga and found similar small crowds. The party was indeed weak among the population. All they knew was the symbol of the hoe, which represented the DP. We realized that ours would be an uphill task to introduce the people to the symbol of the 'open hand' which was that of the UPC. At the same time we were mindful of the new party, which had been launched in Kampala by the Minister of Regional Cooperation, Mr. Yoweri Museveni, and the party was called Uganda Patriotic Movement [UPM]. Majority of the leadership were the youths. This new party attracted the former UPC youth wingers who were looking for new ideas, and wanted to change from the old UPC. They recruited all those who did not have any party affiliations.

The traditional parties UPC and DP were formed on religious grounds, therefore all the moderates who felt that they could not go to DP just because they were Catholics or go to UPC because they were Protestants ended up joining the UPM. This is where we found the Hon. Crispus Kiyonga. The 1980 elections in Kasese were yet to take an interesting turn as the Rwenzururu movement took control of the campaigns. After our meeting with residents of Kyarumba, I was summoned to the king's palace. A man named Yohana Ngike came specifically to lead me to the palace. I was to meet with the Irema Ngoma first, to introduce myself and secondly, to inform the King about my capabilities as a prospective Member of Parliament who would represent the Kingdom and thirdly, to explain to the King what I intended to do for the people. I climbed the mountains for the first time with Ngike. We moved through Kisinga up to Kalingwe and then Kahindangoma where I met the first road block as a sign that the King would be in the neigbourhood. I was to see the King for the first time. I did not know how he looked like. I met a young energetic man sitting on red stool surrounded by two other men whom I later found out were bodyguards. We held a mutual meeting, and we understood each other. I found him to be a sweet, warm middle-aged man. I told him my vision for the district and I found that we shared a lot in common. We discussed the lack of educated people in our district; I explained to him that it was all because we did not have schools. He spoke some little English, but most of our conversation was held in Lukonzo. After our short discussion, we had lunch together comprised of Bundu and goat meat. I was never allowed to see the palace nor the cabinet. Whether they existed or not remained a myth as has been to many, including the present governments.

When I came back, we moved to Bwera and found the former member of NCC Dr. Henry Bwambale being confronted by the Rwenzururu soldiers telling him to stop confusing people about parties. Bazira suggested that we hold a joint meeting with Dr. Bwambale to iron out our differences and look at developments that we wished to bring to Kasese through a joint initiative. Bazira suggested that we field candidate belonging to one party, which was the UPC, but Henry refused. Bazira was prepared to forward Dr. Bwambale's name to the Rwenzururu leaders to represent Kasese North. But Bwambale did not accept to do politics with the Rwenzururu leadership. We continued to align ourselves with the Rwenzururu leaders and encouraged them to tell the people that only one party could solve the problems of our district. We told them that in the past UPC did not handle the Rwenzururu issues just because we did not have representatives within the Party. The time was now since we had identified the problems and we had a party, which had promised to address them. We informed the king's Privy Council that they had been allowed to have a District Commissioner who was a Mukonzo as well as having chiefs from within their ranks. We also informed them that there would be no government which would allow them assume the jobs they held if they did not have elected representatives within their ranks to defend them. And it was obvious that any government other than UPC would dismiss them from their jobs because they were not qualified for those jobs. We then informed the masses that if this political partnership did not materialize the war would resume, and the peace that was being enjoyed would evaporate in thin air. This was a positive campaign tool for the UPC and us. The representatives of the Rwenzururu movement carried this message across the district with the UPC candidates on their sides.

When we came to Kasese Township, we found a mixture of parties, tribes and naturally with this multi-ethnic grouping, confusion emerged. The town had more people informed about party politics than the villages where we had been. It was therefore difficult to just tell the people that we would go with one party. The Uganda Patriotic Movement was already mobilizing most non-Bakonzo voters to join. The Democratic Party was particularly strong here because most businessmen in the township were either from Toro or Bushenyi districts. It was common knowledge that the Batoro were traditional supporters of the Democratic Party. It was at this time that further consultations were necessary between the Rwenzururu leadership and the two of us. A meeting was held in Saad hotel in Kasese where Irema Ngoma sent his Prime Minister Mr. Yeremiya Muhongya. The District Commissioner Mr. Blasio Maate chaired the meeting. He was to be the returning officer and one of his tasks was to ensure that elections were conducted in a peaceful environment. At this meeting in Saad Hotel, the Rwenzururu Prime Minister delivered a message from Irema Ngoma. The message was that: "Rwenzururu movement and their subjects will vote for Uganda Peoples' Congress". The Prime Minister urged the local leaders to adhere to the 'king's call. All chiefs were to preach the message of UPC even though they did not know what UPC stood for. There was disagreement as to how this message was to be disseminated. However, the Prime Minister promised that the Rwenzururu movement would send agents or emissaries who would attend every public rally to ensure that only the UPC was introduced to the people. During this meeting, Dr. Henry Bwambale objected to this method. He subsequently walked out of the meeting and vowed to disassociate himself from the decisions of this meeting.

In August 1980, the king's emissaries stood on the Boma ground of Kasese Township and declared that all non Bakonzo especially the Batoro were to leave the district within seven [7] days. Because chiefs from the Rwenzururu ranks manned the sub counties, this declaration would be enforced without delay. The police was rendered useless because former Rwenzururu soldiers manned the local administration police. The three king's emissaries went to Rukoki, Maliba, Hima and Kicwamba announcing the same massage of expelling the Batoro within 7 days. There was commotion in the district as we saw people leaving Kasese town in an exodus style. Meanwhile on the other side in Fort Portal, the Batoro leaders announced the same. All Bakonzo were to leave Fort Portal in 7 days. This mostly affected were the church priests. They were the only group working in Toro churches. There were no business people from Kasese who would be in Fort Portal. We saw a handful of priests leaving Toro and coming to Kasese their homeland. At that time we still had one diocese called the "the diocese of Rwenzori" where Bishop Yonasani Rwakaikara was the Right Reverend. The Rt. Rev Eustace Kamanyire would later replace him.

At this point it was almost a scandal that the central government could not control the situation. Bazira in his effort to avoid a bloody confrontation among the Bakonzo, had hoodwinked the central government by systematically facilitating the Rwenzururu leadership to take control of the entire district. The district commissioner who could order the police to intervene was handicapped because he paid more allegiance to the "king" although he represented the President of the Republic of Uganda. The central government in Kampala sent two ministers to try to resolve the situation. Minister Akena P'ojok was assigned the responsibility to come and quell the situation. Hon. Akena P'ojok met with the Rwenzururu leaders separately before he met with the political leaders. The Rwenzururu leaders plainly told him that the Batoro had to leave because they were going to overwhelmingly vote for the Democratic Party. Subsequently they were expelled to go to their homeland where they traditionally voted DP. The Minister appealed to the Rwenzururu leaders to rescind their decision and stop the exodus. Mr. Akena proceeded to Kabarole to meet with the Batoro leaders to tell them the same massage to stop the exodus. The situation returned to normal after two weeks of total confusion and turmoil. Those who had gone did not return, and those who were not gone yet, either went eventually or decided to stay and keep a low profile.

The Rwenzururu leaders had made their point, any non-Mokonzo who campaigned for DP or UPM would face retribution. Because Bazira was always on public rallies where the message of expulsion was being delivered, it was conveniently assumed that Bazira expelled the Batoro from Kasese district. This was not true because all the three candidates of the Uganda Peoples' congress were at all rallies; therefore it was wrong for the blame to be placed on one individual, Amon Bazira. The only reason why the assumption was sustained was because Bazira commanded more authority as a former Director General of National Intelligence than any other person in the district plus it was through his scheme that Kasese had been controlled by the Rwenzururu authorities instead of the central government. At one of the rallies for example, Dr. Henry Bwambale was present, and as a former member of the National Consultative council, NCC, he was never associated with the Batoro exodus. During one of the meetings in which the Rwenzururu message of Batoro expulsion was spoken at Katwe, Mr. Yohana Ngike was arrested. He was put in a police cell at Katwe police station, and one policeman, a mutoro by tribe got a hammer and drove a six-foot nail into his head. He died instantly. This case was never investigated and no one was charged for this heinous crime. He was buried with this nail still in his head.

That episode of the exodus passed. The situation slowly returned to normal and campaigns resumed after the government minister had returned to Kampala.

During Independence day celebrations on 0ctober 9th 1980 the Minister of Information Hon. David Anyoti represented the government. He came with a message of reconciliation. He called on the people to live together, vote together and vote for a government that would be committed to their promises. David Anyoti moved on to Fort Portal to address the same rally. We moved on with him. As soon as Bazira arrived, the crowd started calling him the "lion" of Kasese as they booed him. We were however given the platform to greet the people. We later left before Anyoti made his speech. The situation had gradually returned to normal. After the mediation by Hon. Akena P'ojok, political parties were allowed to campaign freely in the district.

We had several candidates conducting political campaigns in several townships. The two other political parties that were DP and UPM had not done their primary elections for fear of what Rwenzururu had announced. They had very little time to organize themselves. One of the hot spots was that in Kasese town centre. This was a heavily populated area with various political opinions. The struggle was between DP and UPM because the UPC already had a candidate endorsed by the Rwenzururu movement. His name was Adam Musa Kisughu [RIP]. Kasese south was to be represented by Amos Kambere and Kasese west was to be represented by Amon Bazira. As soon as the door was open for political campaigns, Kasese north, which had the township, had several candidates emerging as potential contenders for the Kasese north seat. Kasese north had just seen their first graduate by the name of Jorome Mbura Muhindo[RIP]. He started as a member of the Uganda Patriotic Movement just like all young people were. He later crossed into the DP because the politics turned sectarian when the people of Busongora demanded that they need a candidate born in their county to represent them. They said they were tired of being represented by people from Bwera. In fact Bwera provided the most educated persons in the district just because the only junior secondary school was in Bwera. At this time the constituency of Kasese North was all out for grabs. The UPM had a candidate there who was from Bwera, Dr. Chrispus Kiyonga; the DP were planning to field Mr. Victor Muhindo who came from Mundongo Bwera, and the only educated person born in Kasese North was Jorome Mbura Muhindo who was at this time a known member of UPM. So there was tremendous confusion in this constituency.

The Democratic Party demanded that the party executive in Kasese send their candidates names to Mr. Bwengye in Bushenyi. Bwengye was the DP Secretary General. A delegation of DP members left Kasese at night to meet with Bwengye in order to explain to the DP secretariat the dilemma they were facing at nomination. The DP local executive wanted to field Dr. Henry Bwambale in Bwera against UPC's Amon Bazira. They wanted to field Victor Muhindo in Kasese North against UPC's Adam Kisughu. The DP delegation was comprised of Mr. Ngelese of Bwera, Mr. Constantine Syauswa of Bwera and none from Busongora. The local Kasese north people wanted their own Mbura Muhindo to be the candidate and convinced him to cross from the UPM and join DP because it was the stronger party and since he was a catholic, the voters would readily accept him. In fact, Kasese had grown staunchly catholic and violently anti UPC. This left Kiyonga without opposition in his own UPM party. He was therefore returned unopposed in the primaries in Kasese North. The struggle for the leadership of the DP in Kasese North escalated when the indigenous Basongora people forwarded the name of Mbura Muhindo to the DP Secretariat. Unfortunately Francis Bwengye did not accept this nomination because he was aware that Mbura Muhindo had just crossed from UPM and would not attract votes as Democratic Party candidate. Meanwhile as the struggle for leadership was raging on, the UPC had their own struggles in the same constituency. Kasese town had a person from Lango who vied for the seat in Kasese North as UPC candidate. His name was Mr. Patrick Olugo. He was generally supported by the non-Bakonzo in the town. He was sure poised to win. This did not happen because the Rwenzururu movement did not allow primaries in the UPC. They had three appointed candidates and that was final. We were only going to face the candidates from other parties. Mr. Olugo then consented to become only the UPC chairman and was deputized by Christopher Balyebuga. A meeting was quickly held again in the Saad hotel on the eve of the nominations. Patrick Olugo assured the Rwenzururu delegation of his support for Adam Kisughu and encouraged his youth wingers to support the candidature of Adam Musa Kisughu. While we were in that meeting, Mr. Hasan Katigiti brought a note which read that the DP delegation had returned from Bushenyi and Mr. Victor Muhindo had been confirmed as the DP candidate for Kasese North. We expected that the weaker and indigenous candidate, Mr. Mbura Muhindo would be recommended. This did not please Mr. Patrick Olugo. He instructed his youth wingers to arrest the DP candidate, lock him up in Rukoki until nominations were over. Mr. Paul Rwibende, the saza chief would be in charge of this operation to ensure that the DP candidate was released after the nomination closed. Mr. Patrick Olugo with his youth wingers came down from the meeting. He left Amon Bazira, Blasio Maate, the Rwenzururu delegation and I still in the meeting trying to lay a strategy about the nomination which was to happen the following morning. Early in the morning when Patrick Olugo came down by the hotel he found Mr. Victor Muhindo having a meal with Mrs. Henry Bwambale. Patrick Olugo sat in the hotel eating area a few tables away from Victor. Victor Muhindo was an Assistant District Commissioner in Rukungiri District and he did not know who Olugo was, and what role he played in the politics of Kasese Township. He was also the first Mukonzo to become an Assistant District Commissioner. He had served in Mbale before transferring to Rukungiri district. The youth wingers picked Mr. Victor Muhindo; using a high jacked pickup truck, took him away while Olugo watched. When we asked Patrick Olugo what had happened, he told us that the Democratic Party candidate had been taken to Rukoki. This was the morning of nomination. Olugo further explained that Victor would be free after the nominations.

The district commissioner having been delayed in the meeting for at least two hours did not start the process on time as had been stipulated by law. His office was supposed to open at 9:00am but did not open until 10:30 am. Rwenzururu leaders indirectly held the District Commissioner Mr. Blasio Maate hostage for two hours. During this time they were giving him instructions to make sure that he nominates the UPC members first before any other candidate.

Each candidate was supposed to come in with at least 9 people nominating them. These people were supposed to sign nomination papers before the process was completed. Nomination was allowed within three hours from the start of nomination. At this point the process was in the hands of the District Commissioner, also called the returning officer. He did not know what had happened to the DP candidates. By 9:30am the UPC candidates had assembled at the District Commissioner's office ready for nomination. The UPM candidate, Dr. Kiyonga was present with his team ready for nomination. The Democratic Party was still confused as to who was going to be nominated. Two names had been submitted to the Party secretariat in Bushenyi. However, one of the named candidates Mr. Victor Mihindo was missing. Confusion arose as Mbura Muhindo arrived with his team with members ready to nominate him while the members who had come to nominate Victor were also around the office. Dr. Henry Bwambale, Mr.Peter Kato and other members of the Democratic party were still working out a strategy of preventing Jerome Mbura Muhindo from being nominated, but did not know that even their star candidate was missing. The office was crowded with lots of onlookers. Before Mr. Maate could open his office, a group of DP supporters arrived in Peugeot station wagon looking for Mr. Steven Baluku. Noticeable among this gang was Matovu, Kawoya and Ngelese. They demanded to arrest Steven so that he takes them where Victor Muhindo had been taken. They pin pointed Steven Baluku out because he was known staff of the office of the President otherwise known as the secret police. When I saw this confusion, I quickly commandeered a salon car that belonged to the driving school. I told him to drop me down town on Speke Street where Bazira was having last minute briefs with his supporters as they had traveled all the way from Bwera to nominate him. When I arrived on Speke Street, I informed Bazira of the commotion that was happening at the DC's office. We quickly jumbed in Bazira's 120Y Datsun yellow in color Reg. UWR 150. As soon as we arrived at the office, the crowd had increased and Steven Baluku was being dragged in the station wagon. Because he was tall giant with some military training, they did not manage to squeeze him in the rear door as he was resisting furiously. Bazira, the former Director General of intelligence jumped out of his car, pulled out his private pistol and as soon as Matovu and Kawoya saw the "big man" with a pistol, they let Steven go. He had lost all the buttons of his shirt during the struggle. Bazira tried to move towards the office, and Mr. Ngelese confronted him and asked him whether he knew where they had taken Victor, because he was due for nomination. Bazira ignored him and moved on fast to try and disperse the crowd. His pistol fell from his hands, then he picked it and stuffed it back around his waist below his jacket. He really showed off his ability as a former head of a security service. This was the first time people saw his pistol in public. He did not return to Speke street. His supporters were already at the office, ready to nominate him. At this time, the DC opened his office and Bazira was the first to get in. Just in time. He was dully nominated. I was the second to squeeze in. There was such a struggle because we were all chasing time. It was first come, first served. I was duly nominated. As I was getting out, Dr. Kiyonga was right on the door with his supporters and he too was duly nominated. After Kiyonga's nomination, Adam Musa got in and was barely nominated as there was no more time left. In fact the district commissioner would have said no to Adam, but this was a Rwenzururu star candidate. By the time the DC was done with Adam, it was way beyond the legal time for nominations. Dr. Henry Bwambale showed up late because he had been informed by his supporters that there was trouble at the DC's office and that one of the candidates of the DP was missing. Since he was the chairman of the district he was trying to sort things out by getting a substitute in place. However, as he arrived, Mr. Mbura Muhindo was standing outside the office, and frustrated that he could not make the time even when he was right there watching every candidate get nominated. One thing to note here was that the DP district executive did not endorse a UPM convert to stand on the DP ticket. They were struggling to find another alternative to Victor should he not show up for nomination. The bad news was that indeed he did not show up. Instead of taking him to Rukoki County headquarter to be in custody of Paul Rwibende, the Kasese north youth wingers took him to Kichwamba so that he does not find easy transport back in time for nomination. It is believed that some unknown people held him there. He was released late at night and we were informed that he could not find his way to the main road to Kasese. He stumbled into the Toro side of the border, and while he was asking for directions he spoke in Rutoro language because he knew he was on the Toro side of the border. Some Rwenzururu solders who were guarding the border found him and he spoke to them in Rutoro. It was understood that those soldiers stabbed him like they did to many Batoro people and buried him in a shallow grave. The next day we were informed that

Victor had been found dead; his body was exhumed and taken to his home village in Mundongo, Bwera. The bitterness that followed here was unimaginable. To make matters even worse, no member of the Democratic Party was nominated, which meant that they would not field any candidates for the elections. This brought heavy resentment among the entire population. As a protest vote, the entire district vowed to vote for the Uganda Patriotic Movement because this was the innocent party in this affair.

In Kasese south the DP candidate was Mr.Peter Kato, he was at the office, but because of the confusion that had erupted, and he too could not beat the clock. This meant that Kasese South and Kasese West had returned their candidates unopposed. The real election then was in Kasese north. We had Adam for UPC and Chrispus for the UPM. As I mentioned, a protest vote was imminent. There was massive rigging by members of the DP who stole votes for UPM. Many UPC voters were intimidated that Mr. Adam at certain polling stations polled 10 votes while UPM had polled over 1,000 votes. This happened in ridings which did not even have the population that warranted the votes collected. A voters' register was never used in Kasese North as voters came as far as from Bwere to exercise their democratic right to vote. A sympathy vote earned Dr. Kiyonga a constituency. UPM members from Kasese West and South who did not have a chance to vote in their areas came to Kasese North. This probably explains why Dr. Kiyonga was the only UPM candidate elected in the whole Country.

As a final result, Dr. Chrispus Kiyonga was elected member of Kasese North constituency, although he too came from Bwera. Dr. Henry Bwambale filed a law suit against the Uganda Peoples' Congress. He filed his suit on behalf of the entire district, but the case was thrown out of court by the judge because he needed to file on behalf of his constituency not the district. He lost on technicalities.

Elections were held on December 10, 1980 and after Christmas it was time for us to go to the capital city Kampala to be sworn in as Members of Parliament.

In January, I met with Hon. Chrispus Kiyonga elect, discussed with him the strategy of developing our district. He was not happy the way Rwenzururu interfered in the politics of the district. We discussed with him the development of the town ship, I remember he collected and shared with me some statistics from the town clerk office regarding taxation in the general market. We debated about how much money the market in Kasese town council collects in revenue for the town and how that money could be used to develop the town centre. This was truly the way forward for two members of parliament planning together matter of development. We wondered why the town center was not tarmac in spite of all the revenue that is collected from the market vendors and the entire business community in the township; and yet the town clerk's office including the town clerk were extremely rich.

Kiyonga had been my mentor at one point when he was at Makerere University he had encouraged me to pursue Higher School Certificate and at one point promised that he would make it a point that he helped me get admitted into the Faculty of Commerce at Makerere University. Although he was in the Medical Faculty, he promised that with my combination of HEG, [history, economics and Geography] he would use his influence on campus to get me admitted. I again met with Dr. Kiyonga in February in Kampala when I was preparing to go for swearing in. I met him on Kampala road near Uganda House, which hosted the headquarters of UPC; I asked him whether he was considering coming to parliament for the swearing in ceremony. He was very adamant about this. At one point he told me he was not interested in joining a parliament where he was the only member of a political party. His own party leader Mr. Kaguta Museveni had lost to Mr. Kutesa, a member of the Democratic Party. Around February 6 to February 10, 1981 the suburbs of Kampala were rocked with gunshots under unexplained circumstances. In March of 1981, the leader of the UPM party retreated to the bush to fight the elected government. After the swearing ceremony in February, I moved to Kasese to start a crusade that would see an explosion in education.

Chapter 12

EDUCATION:
THE PREREQUISITE FOR DEVELOPMENT

1981 was the year in which the Kasese leaders would sit down together regardless of their party affiliations to discuss the causes of the district's backwardness. As a former teacher, the responsibility was upon me to organize the local leaders, the civic leaders and the politicians to constitute ourselves into a committee to look into the history of education in our area. On one occasion, we invited the Minister of Education Prof. Isaac Ojok and the Minister of Transport and Communication, Mr. Mugenyi. They travelled by train from Kampala to Kasese. We wanted the Minister of Transport to have a feel of the train as it was the gateway to Education for this district and we invited the Minister of Education with him to discuss improvement and the upgrade of Saad secondary school. Mr. Enoch Muhindo and the two members of Parliament from Kasese came as well as the District Commission at the time, Mr. Senyonga who represented Mr.Blasio Maate to welcome the Ministers at Saad Secondary School as seen in the picture above.

In 1976 Amin Dada allowed the moslems from Mpodwe to open the first Secdondary School. It started from the premises of Kisinga Primary School. After two years, the school moved to its present location at Kiburara. The sole financier of the school was Magdad Saad, with money left by his late father Hajji Saad. By the time Amin fell, the school was still a private school. In 1979 during Binaisa's rule, Bazira and Henry Bwambale met with the Minister of Education and secured government aided status for the school. A school lorry was also secured. This was the only secondary school in the area.

Subsequently, when we, the politicians met as leaders, we resolved to promote education by opening up more secondary schools and expanding the existing primary schools. When Mr. Adam Musa failed to make it to parliament, he resumed his old job as District Education Officer. We worked together to open and upgrade the existing primary schools. In 1981 I held a meeting at Kyarumba trading center and called upon business men to donate their money towards opening a secondary school in that area. After that meeting one businessman Mr. Ezroni Syajjabbi volunteered to donate five thousand [5,000/-] Uganda shillings. This was what was needed to show to the Ministry of Education that Kyarumba people were capable of operation a private school. I went with this man to Kampala and met with the Minister of Education Prof. Isaac Newton Ojok. At the time I explained to the Minister the injustice that had happened to the district in the past. I explained the recent history and the willingness of the Rwenzururu movement to assist in making sure that the schools we were about to open would be secured. The Minister did not only grant private school status, he actually approved partial government assistance. This was the birth of Mutwanywana Secondary School. The name Mutanywanaa was borrowed from Mr. Yofesi Masereka, a prominent business man in Kasese town who had showed willingness to help any upcoming development project. This brought the number of secondary schools to two. In the same year 1981 the District Education Officer Mr. Adam led a delegation to Kampala to see the Minister. They demanded that a Secondary school be opened in Kasese North Constituency. The minister agreed to have Rwenzori High School opened as a government school. So, within one year in political office we had a secondary school to each constituency even when Kasese North did not have a representative in Parliament. These schools were purely parents initiated with guidance from the members of parliament. The following year, 1982 the parents of Bwera sub county met with their Member of Parliament Mr. Amon Bazira and expressed the wish to have a secondary school in their area. They argued that if Kyarumba, which was considered a land-locked village [cupboard], can open a secondary school, why wouldn't Bwera do the same? The MP relented and met with the Minister of Education to explain the need for an additional secondary school. At this time, we did not even have enough teachers to run these schools. The only school that had been around for some time was Saad Secondary School. We were therefore depleting the oldest school of qualified teachers. We had already convinced the late Mr. Lazarus Muhindo to leave Saad Secondary School where he was the science teacher to come to Kyarumba and head Mutanywana Secondary School. When Rwenzori High School opened, Mr. Mbayahi Jethro had just finished his degree in Education from the University of Nairobi. He became an easy target to spot for Rwenzori High School.

In 1982, when Bwera opened we had to fish again from Saad secondary and **removed** Mrs. Loice Bwambale to come and head the school. After making significant development at the school, she left the school to become the first Woman to represent Kasese in the National Parliament; the Constituent Assembly. Fearless as she was, many critics referred to her as the "Kasese iron lady" because she withstood the pressures of men who wanted to unseat her.

Ours was just a crash program; we did not care whether only the Headmaster would be the only qualified teacher. We were just after having secondary schools in place and the rest would take care of themselves as the situations dictated. In 1983 the parents of Karambi called for a meeting with their Member of Parliament. He was not available at this time because he was on an overseas trip to Iraq. He authorized me to meet with his constituents on his behalf. I went to Karambi. During this meeting, the hot topic was a need for a secondary school in Karambi Sub County. I said yes to the idea and made arrangements to meet with the Chairman of the Parents Association. We went and met the minister of Education and requested for a secondary school. It was granted on partial government aid. Thereafter, we looked for a Karambi graduate to head the school. We landed on Mbusa Joseph who was my college mate. Mr. Mbusa was not the most qualified for the job but he had exceptional leadership qualities and was capable of heading a secondary school. By the end of 1983 we had had five [5] secondary schools. The opposition leaders heavily criticized us. They argued that we were opening secondary schools on the primary schools premises, something they felt was unacceptable. They also said we did not have qualified teachers to run the school. We decided to ignore their criticisms, as this would deter us from opening more schools. One thing we saw as a positive thing was that each time we opened a school around a primary school premises, there was immediate expansion, as the parents worked hard to put up extra buildings to replace those that were being used by the secondary school. Our primary target was that if by 1984 we have had at least five secondary schools, we would have 200 students sitting for their O'level exams. This would be for sure, 100% Bakonzo kids as they were yearning for education. And this was the plain truth as we offered no apologies for this percentage. It had never happened before for our district to have 200 kids sitting for their senior four exams. It is at this time that I would like to acknowledge with gratitude the efforts put in by the teachers who were hired to execute this plan. All the teachers who worked hard during this time deserve to be acknowledged for the tireless effort they put in to educate these young Bakonzo kids during the most difficult educational circumstances. I know some have passed on like the late Lazaro Muhindo RIP and Jerome Mburamuhindo, while others have left teaching to take on political responsibilities; they need to be recognized as well.

In 1984, I held a meeting with the Permanent Secretary in the Ministry of Education to negotiate for at least two schools that would offer Higher School Certificate. It was necessary to plan ahead as to where our O'level graduates would go. During this year we had invited the Ministers of Education Hon. Philemon Mateke and Prof. Isaac Ojok who had visited the district and were impressed at what we had achieved in a span of three years. They had presided over fundraising functions at Mutaywana Secondry School, Saad Secondary school and Bwera Secondary school. Prime Minister the Hon. Otema Alimadi had also been a guest of honour at some of the functions such as the fundraising at Kagando hospital and had also visited Rwenzori High School. We had invited as many cabinet ministers as we could, **and the message had been received with surprise to see that we were only having our first secondary schools since independence**. When I requested for two schools to offer high school certificate, the response was positive. In 1984, Mutanywana Secondary School opened an Arts class for senior five. Saad Secondary school as well was allowed to open up an Arts class for senior five. The reasoning was if we were going to have at least 200 students sitting for their O'levels, we would have some students who might not be admitted into senior 5 in those 'prestigious' well established schools. We thought that if we had our own schools offering high school certificate, there was a possibility of at least out of 200 students, we might conservatively have 50 joining high school certificate classes while others with lower grades might be admitted into other post secondary institutions. If 50 joined senior five, at least by the end of the two years, we would have perhaps 25 students making it to the University. As the trend was in the past, we always had a few who were admitted into other schools especially in boarding schools. We could probably have another 10 to 15 students from these schools being admitted to the University. So the hope was that at least by 1986 we would have at least 30 to 40 students from Kasese being admitted to Makerere University. This number would increase every year as the facilities and the quality of teaching improved. I did not stay in the country to see this happen but statistics will show that from 1986, the explosion into education was evident and the celebration of this literacy has resulted into quality manpower in the district. The year 1984 was when many activities happened around education. In 1983 Parliament nominated me to join a group of 3 other MPs to attend an inter- parliamentary conference in the city of Geneva, Switzerland. While there, I met an American senator and a Canadian Member of Parliament with whom I discussed the strategy we were using to improve education in our area. They shared with me their own experiences before they received their freedom from the British. They told me about their aboriginal people who were discriminated against in their own land by settlers and how they were also fighting for their rights to education, health care and economic independence. During this discussion, I realized that the Bakonzo had gotten similar experiences, as they were being ruled by the Batoro. My conclusion after meeting with these honorable Senators and experienced legislators was that there was need to engage the government, through dialogue with positive presentations and involve the local people in decision-making. When I returned, I held a meeting with the Speaker of Parliament to give him a feed back from my trip and to discuss an invitation that was extended to me by the US senator. The Speaker, Hon. Francis Butagira plainly told me that parliament did not have enough money to sponsor my trip to the United States. I moved on with my development plans. In that same year, I decided to have a meeting with the citizens of Lake Katwe. I introduced the idea of a Technical College to them. I asked them to think about it and report to me within two weeks. After two weeks I went to Lake Katwe and met the local Uganda People Congress

Chairman, Mr. Bisanku [RIP], together with our Constituency UPC Secretary Mr. Christopher Katemba. They had organized a large gathering like a town hall meeting. We brainstormed ideas about a technical school. We discussed the benefits of such a school, both to our children and to the community. At this meeting we agreed that we should occupy the abandoned building of Kabatoro, which belonged to the Town Council. I had the backing of the parents and the business people of Katwe. By involving the people in making a decision that would affect their community, I felt confident to go to the Ministry of Education to request for a Technical Institution. I explained to the minister that we were going to have many students who will not make it to Higher School Certificate and we must do something for them. Out of the 200 students who would be sitting for O'levels, if 50 went to HSC, we would have more than 100 who would qualify for vocational schools. Since Kasese did not have any of that kind, I convinced the Minister that it was a prudent move to have at least one Technical School. In the same gesture, the Member of Parliament for Kasese West Hon. Amon Bazira was pursuing the same strategy and advocated for a Teachers Training College, which would take again some of the remnants from the 200 students. Our main goal was trying to make sure that we fit up every student in some kind of institution. In 1984, the DEO [District Education Officer] reported that intake in primary school had soared so high that he did not have enough teachers to meet the upsurge. It was like the parents suddenly woke up and sent their children to school. The only Teachers' Training College had just started and was not ready to graduate teachers yet. The existing teachers were mostly grade two and the standards were getting higher and higher.

At this time, I thought of opening another institution, which would produce teachers quicker. A Teachers' College that transformed grade two teachers and upgraded them to grade three was what we needed. This program took only one year. Pragmatically, I had to go to Rwenzori High School to persuade Mr. Jethro Mbayahi to come with me to Kampala. He did not know why I invited him to go with me to Kampala. As we traveled together in my car, we started discussing the possibility of opening up a grade three Teachers' College. Mr. Mbayahi thought Bwera Teachers College was enough to cater for the population, but I told him, that to go to Bwera Teachers College, you had to first pass O'level and stay at college for two year before you could come out and teach. The new Teachers' College would admit already qualified teachers, and would offer upgrade courses. That way we would have within one year a sizeable number of qualified grade three teachers. Mr. Mbayahi saw the point. I went with him to see the Permanent Secretary to the Ministry of Education. I told him that I need a license to operate a grade three Teachers College which would admit only grade two teachers who wanted to upgrade. I informed the Permanent Secretary that I already had a principal; Mr. Jethro Mbayahi. He was right there with me. The Permanent Secretary Mr. Latigo had no choice but to grant the license, because he saw how serious I was and how urgent the need for qualified teachers was; knowing the history we had just gone through as a tribe.

The same day, Jethro Mbayahi was appointed the principal of Kinyamaseke Teachers' College. When he returned from Kampala he met with the parents of Kinyamaseke Primary School to negotiate the use of their buildings while helping to build some for the primary school. Mr. Zephania Bwambale was the chairman of the parents committee at the same time the Vice Chairman of the UPC Constituency Executive Committee. The ideas fell on fertile ground, it was like filling gaps in a puzzle with the right people in place. Each individual we spotted and placed in a school cooperated and worked to the best of their ability. They all understood our recent history and were willing to do what they could to contribute to the success of the process. Mr. Enoch Muhindo was a lecturer at the Kyambogo Teachers' University College; he volunteered to quit that job and came to head Saad Secondary School to bring it to standard, because at the time it now offered A-Level courses. A newly graduated Muranga was to replace Mbayahi at Ruwenzori High School and a technician from Kilembe Mr. Turyagenda was to head the Katwe Technical School. He was not a teacher by profession, but because we could not find a qualified teacher in the technical field we just went in the Kilembe mines and found one who was willing to use his practical experience to pass on technical knowledge. He was a Mukiga by tribe. It was his responsibility to look for other teachers to help him produce successful students in the technical fields. During the same year 1982, Kasese North Constituency was undergoing a bi-election to replace Dr. Kiyonga who had left the country. The constituency was all up for grabs again. Mr. Steven Baluku, Mr. Adam Musa, Mr. Bruno Bwambale and Lt. Tom Baluku were all vying for the same seat and were all belonging to the same party.

At that time I was the Chairman of the district. The District seat was a rotational seat, and in 1982 the Chairman of Kasese South was the Chairman of the district. I was therefore to manage the primary elections. Mr. Amon Bazira put his weight around Mr. Bruno Bwambale because he had just convinced him to abandon DP. The UPC Secretariat put their weight on Lt. Tom Baluku. They even sent a campaigner Mr. Lobidra to come and help Tom win the Kasese North seat. Mr. Steven Baluku and Adam Musa were on their own. I was the neutral figure in this election as the chairman. I probably would have wanted Adam Musa because he kept the flame of the party going and helped in the development of the projects we had started but I left it for the people to decide.

At the primaries, Tom Baluku prevailed and Adam was just the runners up. Steven and Bruno both combined their votes and gave them to Adam, but still he lost to Lt. Tom Baluku. Finally in 1983, Kasese north had a member of parliament. We eventually had our

UPC team complete. I sat with Tom Baluku in his Kasese North parliamentary office and we discussed the possibility of starting another secondary school in Kilembe. My argument was that all the schools we had started were in areas where there were no electricity; therefore, they would confine themselves to Arts subjects.

I proposed to my colleague the MP that we arrange a meeting with the management of Kilembe Mines and ask them to offer some of their buildings in Kyajuki which we could transform into classrooms. I was hoping that since there was electricity and running water in this area, we would open a school that would offer science subjects that required electricity. We visited Kilembe Mines and held a meeting with the General Manager Mr. Mulindwa and explained to him why we needed buildings in Kyajuki for a secondary school. Mr. Mulindwa and his personnel manager Mr. Onyango were positive and promised that they would provide the premises, restructure them to suit classroom environment and would also help to provide furniture for both classes and staff house. To me this was going to be *"the school"*. After this meeting, I went to my office in Kasese; put an announcement on radio Uganda requesting Mr. George Bazirakakye to come to Kasese to meet with me. He did not have a clue as to why he was being called to come to Kasese. He had never been to Kasese. He was a teacher at Kigezi High School as head of the Science Department. We knew each other since I had been a teacher there in 1979. George came to Kasese to meet with an old colleague who had become a Member of Parliament. Within three days, I saw Mr. Bazirakakye arriving at my office by bus from Kabale. I took him to my residence in Kilembe. I called the Member of Parliament, Lt. Tom Baluku to my house and we discussed the possibility of having George head the secondary school in Kilembe. This was great news to him, and he accepted the offer. We traveled to Kampala to meet with the Ministry of Education officials. Lt. Tom Baluku and I met with Prof. Isaac Ojok and explained why we needed a secondary school in Kilembe. We discussed the importance of a school that would offer science subjects because of the facilities for laboratory equipment, which other schools could not afford. The Minister of Education accepted our request, and ordered his Permanent Secretary to appoint George Bazirakakye as the Headmaster with immediate effect. Jerome Mbura Muhindo had been appointed Headmaster of Kasese Secondary School which started in 1982 without political initiative. This was purely a parents' initiated school.

At least by the end of 1984, Kasese District boasted of having 7 Secondary Schools, 2 Teacher Training Colleges, and 1 Technical Institute at Katwe. All these were government-sponsored institutions. Kichwamba Secondary School and Kitolhu Secondary School were the only private schools at the time.

1985 was going to be the election year. Dr. Obote ordered that each constituency in the country be allocated one million Uganda shillings as a development fund. This was the money that was going to start up the campaigns against the Democratic Party. As for Kasese, we were for sure going to win, because we had proved to the population that we were capable of keeping our promises and this is what we could deliver during the second term in office. We had been able to pull the district from one secondary school to ten [10] post primary institutions. The number of primary schools had increased as well. The second term was going to be devoted to clean water projects, Health Centers and Hospitals, good roads and other social services that were necessary for a developing district. Kasese West was already earmarked for a hospital, which was to supplement Kagando, and Kilembe. These two were the only private Hospitals serving a population of over 700,000 people. Peace had returned to the district by the descending of the Rwenzururu leadership in 1982. Uganda Peoples' Congress had transformed the district through dynamic leadership.

Chapter 13

POLITICS AND THE CHURCH: KASESE WAS NO EXCEPTION

The church in Kasese underwent tremendous changes in 1979 when the entire district was governed by the Rwenzururu authorities. The hard hit denomination with this change of political and civil authority was the Anglican Church. During Christmas of 1979 and that of 1980 the Irema Ngoma leadership ordered that all gift collections; tithing and donations should not be given to the diocese headquarters in Fort Portal as was the practice. Instead, he ordered that all collections be handed to the "ministry" responsible for church under the Rwenzururu leadership. Any church that would not comply would face severe punishment. So the Pastors and Church leaders had to comply. Some of the Reverends who were kicked out of Toro during the exodus had been assigned to head small churches. The Rwenzururu leadership demanded that the Church of Uganda authorize the church in Kasese to govern itself in a new and separate diocese from that of Rwenzori, which was governed by Fort Portal. In 1981 Bishop Rwakaikara retired. He was allowed to come and preach his farewell sermons to the Kasese churches on condition that he will not demand for the money collected during Christmas of 1980 to be taken to Fort Portal. The new elected Bishop was Bishop Kamanyire. During his consecration speech, he called the Rwenzururu leaders "rebel" and he appealed to them to surrender the money they withheld so that he could run the affairs of the diocese well. In turn, the Rwenzururu leaders banned him from ministering to churches in Kasese. They said he would be arrested if he dared visit Kasese. Amon Bazira and I attended his consecration ceremony held at the Cathedral in Kabarole. Bishop Kamanyire later appointed me to be his representative on the Diocesan synod representing the churches from Kasese. When we realized that the Rwenzururu leadership would not relent, we invited the Arch Bishop of Uganda Rt. Rev. Silvanas Wani. We arranged a meeting between Irema Ngoma and the Arch Bishop. The meeting took place at the Historic Nsenyi Catholic Parish. The Bishop of Rwenzori Dioces, Rev. Kamanyire, accompanied Arch Bishop Wani, and members of his privy council accompanied Irema Ngoma and on the government side we had the District Commissioner Mr. Blasio Maate. On the political side we had Amon Bazira the MP for Kasese West and Myself as the MP for Kasese South. Canon Steven Mukirane and Ven. Yona Kule represented the local churches. At the meeting, the Rwenzururu delegation emphatically told the arch Bishop that Kasese demanded for a separate diocese. The archbishop responded that a separate diocese would not be achieved by confiscating the money that was meant to run the church affairs. At this time, the pastors in Kasese had gone several months without salaries and most churches were surviving by the mercy of the Lord. The Arch bishop and Irema Ngoma struck a deal. Bishop Eustance Kamanyire was allowed to come and preach in Kasese to prepare the Christians for a separate diocese and the Rwenzururu leaders agreed to release the money in order to pay for the salaries of the Kasese reverends and church leaders. Irema Ngoma demanded that a second Arch Deaconry be established to create room for priests who were kicked out of Fort portal. Among them was the Venerable Yona Kule who had been dean of the Cathedral in Fort Portal and Principal of Bukuku Theological College. The Archbishop agreed to establish a second Arch Deaconry to create a job for Rev. Yona Kule. At this time Rev. Canon Steven Mukirane became the Arch Deacon of Kisinga while Yona Kule became the Arch Deacon of Kasese. A committee was set in place to continue discussions and negotiations to bring to reality the establishment of a separate Diocese. Mr. Muhyana was nominated chairman of that committee comprising of the two Arch Deacons, Steven and Yona plus a few Christians from the Bwera Church. A committee of three was formed to draft a Constitution; the members were Amos Kambere, Ivan Muhasa and the Church lawyer Mr. Nyakana of Fort Portal. As a representative of Bishop Kamanyire on the Diocesan synod, I was charged with representing the views of the Arch Deaconry of Kasese and Kisinga in the synod. I did not even sit on this synod because it did not take long before we got our own diocese. At this time as was always the case like other positions in the district, we did not have anyone qualified to head the diocese. One native Pastor from Kasese was in the United Stated studying. His name was Rev. Zebedee Masereka, an old boy of mine from the National Teachers' College of Kyambogo. Rev. Z. Masereka had graduated from Kyambogo University College, and went off to Nyakasura to become the chaplain for the school. It was from here that he left for the United States on Church Scholarship to study divinity. He already had a Diploma in Education, a Diploma in Theology and was now admitted into a USA Theological College where he graduated with a Masters Degree in Divinity. He came back to be the Dean of the Kabarole Cathedral. By the end of 1982, Bishop Kamanyire had concluded his pastoral visit to Kasese and declared that we were ready for our own diocese.

The stories he received and the reports he got from the Priests convinced him that he could not insist on keeping Kasese under the Rwenzori diocese. We had to go through a process of selecting a Bishop to head the upcoming diocese.

The Province in Kampala had heard from Arch Bishop Wani and the recommendation was that Kasese be granted a separate diocese from Kabarole. The business of selecting a Bishop was left to Bishop Kamanyire's synod. This became my first and last synod meeting to attend. At this synod meeting I was appointed the chairman of the Electoral College. I was therefore to take my seat not as a voter from the Kasese Arch Deaconry, but as a Chairman to oversee the election of a new diocese. The new diocese was to be called South Rwenzori diocese because we already had the Catholic Diocese called Kasese Diocese headquartered in Bunyaruguru. Every archdeaconry was allowed constitutionally to send 9 representatives who would participate in the election. Because Kasese had only two archdeaconries, we had 18 delegates. The rest of the delegates came from other Arch Deaconries of the Rwenzori diocese to participate in the election. In other words, even delegates from Bwamba, Burahya and Bunyangabo Arch Deaconries participated in electing a Bishop for the new diocese of South Rwenzori. As the Chairman of the Electoral College, I did not have the chance to cast my vote, I carried my vote with me as a souvenir. We had three candidates who contested for the position of Bishop. They were Rev. Yona Kule, Rev. Steven Mukirane and Rev. Zebedee Masereka. Only one of the three was really qualified to head a diocese. I conducted the elections in a free and fair fashion. At the end of the day, the Very Rev. Zebedee Kahangwa Masereka was returned as the Bishop of South Rwenzori Diocese. I delivered the results of the vote to the Bishop and the process of establishing a new diocese started. We then left Fort Portal to go and start the preparations of consecrating a new Bishop. Amon Bazira used his business contacts in Kampala to secure for the diocese a new car for the bishop. A small Hyndai light green in color was secured on loan to be paid for by the money that was being held by the Rwenzururu leaders. We negotiated with Kilembe mines to allow the Bishop to live in their quarters at McGowan. We moved to Kampala as a team of three Members of Parliament to invite the President to be a chief guest at what was to be a historic moment in the history of the people of Kasese. Two years prior to this, Irema Ngoma had come down with his entire army and on August 15, 1984 H.E. the President Dr. Apollo Milton Obote would accept our invitation to attend this function, which would be officiated by the Arch Bishop of Uganda, the RT. Rev. Yona Okoth. All the Bishops of the church of Uganda attended this historic function.

I do not think Kasese District will ever have political leaders who will be as busy and involved as we were between 1981 and 1985. We dealt with critical and sensitive issues at the same time keeping the people united and peaceful. There was no evidence of massive loss of life or property during this time. At the same time we did not condone the loss of a few during the early years of our term of office. The district lost Victor Muhindo, Patrick Olugo and Edward Sempebwa under unexplained circumstances; all three were of significant importance. While we mourned these lives, we kept the people united, progressive and productive.

Chapter 14

RWENZURURU: THE FINAL EPISODE

Amon Bazira and I had been involved right from the time Kasese fell to the Rwenzururu Movement after Idi Amin. A relationship was created during the time we were negotiating with the 'king', first to stop the taxation that had been going on for years and second to surrender the church money that had been confiscated during the Christmas of 1979 and 80. We held several meetings with the 'King's Privy Council' and the King Irema Ngoma himself. Bazira was not very fluent in Lukonzo, and one of the words that used to give him hard time and created good humor amongst the kings entourage was; "*emitheghekere*". He used to pronounce it the way a mutoro would say it. And whenever he said words like "*emitheghekere ya banyabuthoki*" there was laughter all the time lending humour to the discussion. I was the fluent guy and did most of the talking. Bazira always came prepared with money because one of the demands that was put on the table when he convinced them to abandon the taxation policy, they said; "how do we pay the soldiers, Members of the Privy Council and Ministers?" Bazira always gave them substantial sums of Uganda shillings. He did not tell me how much it was each time, but I could see it was a sizeable chunk of money. They were happy, because they had money to replace whatever they had been collecting from people.

We also convinced them to stop collecting "*obuhunga*" [cassava floor] from citizens. It had been common practice for them to collect cassava flour from every village to feed the Rwenzururu soldiers. Again, as we gave them some money, they accepted to stop this practice. On each market day, every fish vendor was to submit at least 2 tilapia fish to chiefs because the Rwenzururu leaders wanted to feed well. Again, this was a practice we brought to an end. There were so many things the movement was doing which were displeasing to their own people. These had to stop as a result of our efforts. We made sure that we closed every avenue in which they squeezed the common man. That is why when you talk of the UPC leadership of the 1980s, people will remember the agony that was removed from them by eliminating the unnecessary suffering that was a common practice by Rwenzururu soldiers. Amon Bazira and Amos Kambere as pictured above are credited for stopping those encumbrances.

After the meeting at the historic Nsenyi parish with the Archbishop, we organized another meeting to strike a major deal for the King to descend from the mountains and relinquish his authority to the central government. In 1981, we made several trips to Kalingwe and Kahindangoma to meet with Charles Wesley Irema Ngoma. At each of these meetings we had the District Commissioner Mr. Maate with us as a symbol and gesture of how the government was seriously interested in negotiating with the Rwenzururu movement. Dr. Obote had given us the mandate to negotiate on behalf of the government. Before we left parliamentary buildings we told President Milton Obote that the first UPC government lost a lot of money, lives and property. They did not succeed in eliminating the movement. We further reiterated that General Amin with his mighty army, even after giving them the district, did not eliminate them, instead more lives were lost and more money was spent on the army trying to fight a civil rebellion that could have been solved by negotiations. Hence, on our part we had convinced the government that peace talks and a message of reconciliation was the way forward. Before we moved on our final approach, we first agreed among ourselves what we would accept if we were in their shoes. We did some role play here, and one of us pretended to be the 'king". We knew that these people had fought a bitter war for twenty years, and it was time for them to give it up. We therefore started with what we would need if we were in their shoes as we came down for the first time? First, we suggested a house to live in. Secondly, we thought of a car to travel, Third, we thought of how he could earn a living, and next what would the future be like, and finally what title would the king have after stripping him of his "rebel royal" titles. We also asked what would happen to the many soldiers he had recruited into the Rwenzururu army. Obviously, we suggested a house, a saloon car, a bus, a small pickup. In addition, we suggested two commercial buildings in Kasese town to generate income for the entire household, the King already had an Isuzu truck which the army had misused and had to be replaced with a Tata Lorry. After answering these questions, we moved on to climb to the furthest private cave at Kahindangoma. We put these suggestions on the table and asked the 'king' to discuss them with his cabinet. At first, they liked the proposals, but then they said these only took care of the King. The questions remained; what about the rest of the leaders, the fighters, etc? We quickly came up with the answer. We suggested that the fighters would be absorbed into the national army, the UNLA and the rest of the 'ministers' would be appointed into local chiefs and other positions within the local government. At this meeting, we were just creating goodwill. We had to go back to our own government and convince the President that all the demands were worth the expenditure, because we would be solving a civil rebellion once and for all. The expenditure would not be equivalent to the loss of lives and property on both the side of the government soldiers and the civilian casualties. Besides, there had been the long existing conflict between the Bakonzo and Batooro which would come to an end. Dr. Milton Obote gave us the green light. He authorized us to arrange a meeting between his army Chief of Staff, his Minister of State for Security and the Irema Ngoma team. At this point we knew we were on the right track and were about to strike the bull's eye. So we made our regular climb via Nsenyi parish, we met with Reverend Father Balinandi, the Parish Priest at the time. He agreed to host the meeting between the Uganda government officials and the officials of the Rwenzururu movement. We made our trek uphill and met with the king. We requested for a meeting in which they would have to put their demands on the table. We told them that the President of Uganda was willing to meet their demands as long as these would bring to an end the civil rebellion and would enable the king to come and live among his people and talk about development and not destruction of lives and property. A day was set for the meeting. We had a compelling reason for the use of political incentives where the king's cabinet would be absorbed within the work force even though most of them might not have been qualified. We were determined to use negotiations and mediation tactics instead of coercion and punishment which had failed in the past. This conflict had deterred development of schools, roads and hospitals. The government was more concerned with quelling the civil rebellion than thinking about development. Conditions for development had to be created, and we were committed to bringing this to a peaceful conclusion in order for us to push our agenda of development through the UPC government.

In early 1982, Major General David Oyite Ojok, Uganda's Chief of Staff, Hon. Chris Rwakasisi, Minister of State Office of the President responsible for Security, made up the government delegation while the Irema Ngoma, Prime Minister Yeremia Muhongya and several members of the Privy Council made up the Rwenzururu delegation.

The District Commissioner of Kasese Mr. Maate, Hon. Bazira and Hon. Kambere represented the local leadership. The meeting was held amidst heavy security provided by the Rwenzururu soldiers. The first check point manned by Rwenzururu soldiers was at Kagando Hospital. Every one who traveled from Kasese, including David Oyite Ojok's guards, was disarmed. All guns were held at that point. The second was at Kiswahili's house at Kisinga Trading center, and the third was 100 meters from the Nsenyi Parish Church. The Uganda Army Chief of Staff saw how the roadways leading to Nsenyi parish were militarized by rebel soldiers in uniforms similar to that of the Ugandan Army.

At one time Rwakasisi whispered to Oyite Ojok that, "can you imagine, you the Nation's Chief of Staff, disarmed? This means you have been stripped off your military authority, you are at their mercy," It sounded like treason and yet it was not, just respect for the Iremangoma's soldiers. It looked like a movie story, and yet it was real. The situation was tense. At Nsenyi parish about 25 soldiers, heavily armed formed what we later knew was a guard of honour. Oyite Ojok was forced to ceremoniously inspect this guard of honour and when Irema Ngoma arrived, they sang the Rwenzururu anthem plus the Uganda National anthem. Irema Ngoma too inspected this guard of honour mounted by his own troops. After this, we went into the meeting room. The tension was relaxed when Rev. Father Balinandi opened with a word of prayer and the meeting started. Rwakasisi welcomed the king from his mountain hideout to the plains, delivered greetings from the President of Uganda. Oyite Ojok delivered greetings from the army commander, General Tito Okello, and promised to deploy the willing and able Rwenzururu soldiers into the National Army.

Irema Ngoma on his part accepted the conditions we had laid on the table. He wanted reassurance from the government that what we had proposed to him would be a reality should he accept to come down peacefully.

He promised to come down and join the government in the struggle of reconstruction and reconciliation. The government in turn, on top of the tangible material items, promised the Omusing*a a scholarship which would give him education opportunities to study* in the United States of America.

Immediately, a day was set as August 15th 1982 when the king and his entire army with their arms would descend the hills of Kahindangoma down to Nsenyi and then to Kasese Boma ground. During this time as we were going on with the negotiations, one of Irema Ngoma's brothers, William Sibibuka, had been held by the army in Mbarara and was being looked after by Lt. Tom Baluku who was assigned to the Western Brigade at Mbarara. Irema Ngoma requested that his brother be released unconditionally. The Chief of Staff David Oyite Ojok promised to look into this matter. He eventually instructed Captain Namiti together with Lt. Tom Baluku to have William brought back to his family. It is from this connection that Lt. Tom Baluku came to be in contact with the King and the Rwenzururu establishment.

On the day of descending down, The District Commissioner and the Members of Parliament went to Nsenyi to welcome the king and his entire army. Two lorries, plus one bus were assigned to transport the entire Rwenzururu army. That night, Irema Ngoma was smuggled by Lt. Tom Baluku assisted by Captain Namiti to spend the night in Mweya Safari Lodge. They managed to do this without the local leaders' knowledge as well as the Rwenzururu Chief of Staff. There was fear that Kinyamusitu who was the Rwenzururu Chief of Staff had refused to comply with the negotiated deal. He vowed to stay in the mountains and continue fighting. There was also fear that Kinyamusithu could harm the king by staging a palace coup. Such suspicions led Tom and Namiti to smuggle the 'king' into Mweya. and delivered him very early in the morning to the foothills near Nsenyi to appear as if he was coming from up the mountains. For the first time, in 20 years, Irema Ngoma first came to Mweya before he officially entered the Peugeot 505, which had been prepared to ferry him to the Boma ground in Kasese. On 15th August 1982, a long motorcade descended on Kasese Boma grounds, carrying the "Bakonzo and Bamba king" with the majority of his arms and ammunitions. It was a day of jubilation as it marked the end of the 20 years of bitterness, the long years of suffering, backwardness, and insubordinations. This was the beginning of progress, the beginning of mature politics that looked at development and not destruction. The ceremony was attended by Uganda government Ministers, Members of Parliament and an estimated 20,000 people. People came from all neighboring districts, including the traditional enemies, Toro district. All come and see the "king" who, for more than 20 years had defied arrest, and kept the army on their feet as well kept politicians and government leaders and Presidents restless.

In a speech prepared for him, Iremangoma had this to say, and I quote: "...We have come down, not as surrender, but to come and join the government, to work and find solutions to our people's problems..." In his book, Rwenzururu 20 years of Bitterness, Bazira contends, I quote: "*"that, finding solutions to our problems had been the primary objectives of the Rwenzururu leadership."* For example he mentions that "Isaya Mukirane believed that there was a sense of superior group position prevailing in Uganda where by some people thought that their tribes were better than the Bayira; a matter that resulted in the subordination of the Bayira and the low political esteem accorded them. He had come to the conclusion that in most cases discrimination was practiced against the Bayira covertly unknown to the victims and that a muyira in Uganda unlike a muyira in Congo begins the race of life with a detectable handicap of discrimination". [Bazira pp 12]. These are some of the issues Irema Ngoma referred to when he said he and his team had come down to dialogue with the government to find solutions to and crash discrimination in all its forms. Some of the issues that were addressed as a result of this decision were notably the creation of a separate diocese for the people of Kasese. Negotiations to have this effected were carried out between the former arch-bishop of Uganda the Most Rev. Salivanas Wani and the honorable members of parliament at the time; the Bishop then of Rwenzori the Rev. Eustace Kamanyire. Progressively two years after Irema Ngoma had came down, on August 15, 1984 the first Bishop of south Rwenzori diocese was installed.

Chapter 15

THE 1985 COUP D'ÉTAT

It was 11:30a.m on July 27th 1985. A close friend of mine came running to my office on Margarita Street in Kasese town. "The government has been overthrown" he reported. You must be kidding, I answered. He insisted and pulled out a transistor radio from his pocket. "Here, listen for yourself!!" As I listened, I heard the voice of Lt. Ochora announcing that the government had been overthrown and that Brig. Bazirio Olara Okello was in charge. I thanked him for the information and it appeared that He was the only one who had so far known about the coup. I picked up my brief case, came slowly down the stairs, to the street. I saw the UPC Chairman Mr. Balyebuga standing casually on the street in a leisurely conversation with Captain Otto. Looking at their body language I realize that they had not heard the news of the take over. I did not want to tell them, because I did not know what the army officer would do, since he was from the Bazirio Okello tribe. I was with my constituency treasurer, I jumped into my red datsun car, took off for Kilembe. While driving to Kilembe I tuned on my car radio and indeed the government had fallen, there was news that the President had fled the country and that the coup was bloodless. I got to my house in Kilembe, my wife was pregnant with our second child. She had gone to Bwera to attend a wedding of our friend Constance Mutooro wedding Mika. I packed my brief case with some money plus a few clothes and attempted to head for Congo boarder immediately. What I feared mostly were the rebels of the NRA whom we had prevented from taking over Kasese and were still encamped around the hills of Bunyangabo and Maliba. We would be easy targets when they get to town.

I jumped into my car and drove, hoping that I would simply drive through and get to the boarder before things get worse. This did not happen. As I drove towards Kasese, I came across a convoy of vehicle all running towards Kilembe and every one I passed waved me to turn back. The indication was that the town was not safe to drive through. The news of the coup had now arrived home and every one was on the run. My treasurer and I made a complete U turn and headed back to Kilembe. When I got back to my house, I parked the car, went into the house to scribble a note to my wife that I was heading for Congo through the mountains. After the note, we started the long climb. When we reached the top of the mountain overlooking Kilembe, where we could still see my house, we stopped and tuned on the transistor radio. We saw NRA soldiers who were hiding among the population coming to my house. They did not loot anything, but entered my bedroom to remove the gun they knew I had. It was Rev. Mutazindwa who came to my house to remove the gun. On the radio, it was being announced that Bazirio Olara Okello was after Dr. Obote, Rwakasisi and Peter Otai. All other Ministers were free. We did not take any chances anyhow. We moved through the hills while monitoring Kampala via the transistor radio. On the second day of the coup, we heard the announcement of the Head of State as that of Gen. Tito Okello and Paul Muwanga was announced as the Executive Prime Minister. At the swearing in of this regime, we heard on the radio, that former Ministers Kanyomozi, Samwiri Migwisa, and Amon Bazira were in attendance. After hearing this news I decided that making the trek to Congo through those thick mountains was not the best decision. I was simply a mere member of parliament and wondered why I should be on the run, when the big shots were being announced as part of the new regime. I decided to stay in my village of Kyarumba until the situation was completely calm. My wife returned from the wedding and was at home. After one week I moved back to

Kilembe to join my wife. The first trouble we encountered was the loss of our house as we were hauled into a small one bedroom house. A soldier who identified himself as Bahindi carried out the operation of getting us out of the Kilembe mines houses. What happened was that, as Tito Okello was sworn in as President he appealed to Yoweri Museven who was in Sweden at the time to come and join hands with him to rule Uganda after Obote. Yoweri Museven while in Sweden was not too anxious to work with the Okellos. He had been fighting them for the past 4 years. He called for negotiations while he ordered his men who were on the run in the west to consolidate their ground. They immediately captured Fort Portal and Kasese and organized massive recruitments. A lot of disgruntled UPDF soldiers who were tired of working with the Okellos, joined in this massive recruitment. That is how we saw people like the Rev. Mutazindwa and NRA officer Bahindi taking control of Kasese under the command of Rwigyema and Kagame at the time. Museven consolidated his grip on the west by using Rwanda as the gateway. He called for peace talks while the Okellos turned around and thought they would defeat while forgetting that they had been at war with Yoweri Museven for four years and failed. President Daniel Arap Moi of Kenya offered to mediate a peace deal, in what many generally called the "peace jokes". They were peace jokes because Yoweri Museveni knew he was negotiating with a regime of illiterate generals with only one brilliant intellectual, the Minister of Foreign Affairs, Mr. Olara Otunu. While the peace talks were going on in Nairobi Museveni was busy acquiring territory by over-running all the cities in the west. His army grew up so fast and it was the most disciplined army Ugandans had seen in many days since Idi Amin left power. The west was peaceful while the central, which was controlled by the Okello soldiers was in a mess; people were in misery, absolutely dominated by sadness, abject poverty and worse off than when Obote was in power. This domination of sadness and misery would go on in Northern Uganda where the Okellos hailed from for more than twenty years. *"Tough price to pay when you overthrow an elected government!"* When Museven finally took control of Mbarara and was heading for Masaka, it became general knowledge that he was not interested in a peaceful settlement. He was not willing to share power with men he had been previously fighting with in Luwero presumably because he did not want to explain much about the atrocities both armies had committed against the people of Luwero and Mubende districts. In Fort Portal, Al hajji Musa Kigongo was in charge with a few cadres helping him sort thing together. Hon. Chrispus Kiyonga returned from his exile home in Kenya and held one of the offices in Fort Portal. As I recall in February of 1985 I had visited Nairobi on business and had wanted to meet with Dr. Kiyonga on personal level. One of the things I wanted to discuss with him was that the UPC government was weakening every day by the conflict between the Langi and Acholi tribes especially in the army. I wanted to give him an inside story of what I knew after the death of David Oyite Ojok and perhaps find out what plans he had to return either to join us or whether he thought their bush war was making any progress that would provide a better alternative should there be a change of leadership between the Acholis and the Langis.

The contact I used from Campus Crusade to get to him reported back to me that Dr. Kiyonga will not meet with me because he feared I could be a spy wanting to kidnap him. Imagine simple civilian Member of Parliament as I was, to arrange a kidnap? This was not possible and not even something I could contemplate on doing. I lost an opportunity to connect with him for I found out later that he was very involved and connected as this became evident, when they took control of

Kasese and Fort portal. I concluded that he was really well connected. Did I regret not seen him in Nairobi? No. Within 6 months, the Okello Regime was overthrown and on January 26, 1986 Yoweri Museveni declared himself President of the Republic of Uganda. He announced a fundamental change with a 10-point program. He announced a cabinet in which the Bakonzo received their first full cabinet Minister. Dr. Chrispus Kiyonga was appointed Minister of Corporative and Marketing. Later, during several reshuffles, he occupied other prominent ministries such as the Finance Ministry, the Internal Affairs Ministry, the Health Ministry [his profession], and now the Defense Ministry. Before the defense Ministry, he was the NRM Secretary General. When God gives, He gives in full. The Bakonzo had for a long time been crying for representation, God opened the door during this period when Museveni was President that their native Kiyonga has had the opportunity to occupy those prominent ministries deservingly since he was the only one who carried the banner of the UPM Party during the 1980 elections. There has often been talk in the corridor of power of people lining up for succession to the job of President. Amama Mbabazi who claimed that Col. Kiiza Besigye had jumped the queque first underscored this. Minister Otafirre later reiterated it. The man who should be close in the so-called lineup for the job should be Kiyonga, but has he shown interest? I don't think so because Kiyonga has not strived to have his life chronicled into the NRM's archives. He eschews the corridors of power by remaining the humble and loyal subject to His Excellency the President. He is the ultimate survivor in the regime where Ministers have come and gone. He is the only Member of Parliament who has held 5 of the most powerful cabinet positions as well as the National Political Commissar. He was in his own words and I quote; "I was the only MP elected on the UPM ticket in 1980 that did not invalidate the cause for which I stood. On the contrary our thinking has blossomed in Uganda. In that case I am on record as the only MP who spear headed the growing of passion fruits and this has assisted many people all over Kasese. In Kampala if you want to get quality passion fruits you ask for those from Kasese. My struggle to revive cotton growing in Kasese is known to everybody. Being the only MP pushing this cause did not stop the fire catching on. I have scored a **first** in many other situations. That is leadership and I will continue leading the way in this regard". [New Vision Jan. 2005]

Dr. Kiyonga has had his positive contributions to the development of the district. Although he has been adamant and skeptical about the re-establishment of the Businga, he has articulated his reasons for rejecting the *Omusinga* while embracing the idea of the *Obusinga*. In the memorandum to the government he contends ... on issue of integrity, politics and representation. ...

The Omusinga Charles has often clashed with Dr. Kiyonga on public rallies as was evidenced on his return which attracted massive numbers of Bayira.

All in all, Dr. Kiyonga has remained a solid representative of his new constituency. At first, he was Member of Parliament representing Kasese North, but when he came back from his exile life, he went to his native Bwera where he has carried out development projects to benefit the people. In 1980 Bwera had two political giants in the names of Amon Bazira and Dr. Henry Bwambale. In 1986 Dr. Kiyonga prepared himself to be the next giant who would replace and carry on the development projects and all the unfinished business in Kasese West. In the 4 years Bazira was the representative, Bwera hospital was just a thought idea to be built on the Hill. Other ideas as put down by the local UPC Committee were water, electricity and development of new schools. In 20 years Dr. Kiyonga has been the representative, Bwera has seen clean water, the hospital has been built and the schools that started in the 1980s have been improved and upgraded. There has been improved security and communication overall. But let us not forget that this representative has held instrumental positions in government, thanks to H.E. Yoweri Museven for the confidence he has continued to bestow on this native son of Bwera. Obote did not do it the first time in 1962 – 70 or the second time 1980-84. The explanation the first time was that the Bakonzo did not vote for UPC therefore he did not find anyone credible and educated enough to be appointed as a minister. The highest position held by a Mukonzo was that of High Commissioner to the UK. When Ezron Bwambale crossed from DP to UPC he was immediately appointed Deputy Minister of Culture and Community Development. A strong message to the voters that they need to have voted for a strong UPC party member in order to secure a cabinet position. In 1980, there was a petition hanging on Amon Bazira filed by the Democratic Party. Obote explained that he did not want his government to be embarrassed if a cabinet minister lost the petition. Plus the elections in Kasese did not appear fair since there was news of misconduct at the returning officer's office. We did not lose the petition though, and Amon Bazira was never appointed full Minister in the four years Uganda Peoples Congress was in government. Bazira however remained very powerful in security circles dating back from the time he was the Director General of intelligence. His cabinet colleagues did not like him either because he was potentially fit for any of their portfolios in case the President decided on a reshuffle of his cabinet. Amon Bazira was assisinated in 1993 in Nairobi Kenya while waging a liberation war against the NRM government. He was the head of NALU, the National Army for the Liberation of Uganda, a rebel movement that operated out of the Congo DRC. This rebel Army ceased to exist after he died in exile. The remnants joined the ADF, alied democratic forces, which were defeated by the government army in 1996.

Chapter 16

FROM PRISON TO PRAISE

In June 1986 when the NRM was fully in power, I did not see any chance of ever joining their political line. I decided to quit politics and start my own school in which my wife would be a teacher and I would be the Sole Proprietor. I had two vehicles, a salon car and a pick up truck. I decided to sell my Salon Nissan Datsun 120Y model to buy a second pickup truck. The reason for this was to use one truck in the construction of the school, while the other was to be used for commercial purposes. I knew I would earn a living while constructing the school. I started carrying bricks. I laid a foundation for four classes and another for a staff house to house at least two teachers. Work was in progress in the whole month of June. My wife enrolled at Canon Apollo College to upgrade her skills to a grade three teacher. When she was gone for one week at Canon Apolo College, I went down town Kasese on my way to the village where my bricks were being prepared. I stopped by the market and was approached by a tall man in plain clothes who introduced himself as John Doe [*not real name*] for purposes of this book. He asked me to drive him to the Kasese district court. He sat in the front seat of my small mini truck, a 120Y datsun pickup. I drove him to the court; not aware that I was driving myself to court. As soon as we reached the court house, he told me, "You are under arrest". I said, "For what?" He dragged me into the court and because he was such a tall giant, I did not resist. As if it was all stage managed, the magistrate was right there in his robes and read the charge to me. "*You are accused of Kidnap*, so you plead guilty or not guilty? In shock, I just replied, "not guilty" your honour Magistrate. "I am therefore **directed** to send you on remand to Mubuku prison right away". I told them I was not aware of the charges against me. They did not give me even a chance to talk to a lawyer nor inform my family. I drove my car with this tall man to Mubuku prison. To me this was the real kidnap; I was not allowed to leave my car with anybody. Everything appeared to have been pre-arranged; I found the head of the prison institution, a senior superintendent of prisons waiting for me. He ordered one of the prison warders to register me, strip me of my civilian clothes and dress me with prison uniform which was dirty and infected with lice. I was humiliated, undressed and dressed in prison dirty white cotton uniform. I complied with the orders and at this point I knew that the tall man was not joking, it was real and I was now a prisoner. News circulated in Kasese town that I had been arrested and two people immediately came to see me while still at Mubuko prison. Mr. Yofesi Masereka came to see me and drove my small pickup truck back home. The second one was the Bishop of south Rwenzori diocese. He prayed for me with an assurance that "**with God nothing is impossible**" and promised that he would immediately travel to Fort Portal to get my wife from school so she can take care of family business. Her teaching career was now doomed and her two little boys' future was unpredictable. As well, it was obvious that the school project was dead. My political career as the youngest Member of Parliament had vanished with the coup the previous year. My whole life was turned upside down. *This was the long road God was preparing for me in order to transform me and to eventually turn me to Himself and begin to know Him and love Him.*

Phil. 1 vs. 6 says " he who started a good work in you will see to it that it is completed for the glory of His Kingdom." [Paraphrased from NIV]

There was an immediate unrest in the prison quarters. Inmates were anxious to see me and were probably prepared to scold me or even whip me as the practice was. I stayed at what I later came to know as the quarter guard for more than two hours before I was allowed to join other remanded prisoners. There was unfounded rumor that the remnants of Rwenzururu rebels headed by Kinyamusitu were going to storm the prison in order to forcefully release me. Because of this rumor, I was quickly transferred to the notorious Katojo prison in Fort portal. This was considered maximum-security prison in Western Uganda. Two weeks later, I was produced before the High Court Magistrate in Fort Portal and the same charges were read to me. I was again remanded in Katojo. Three weeks later Milton Bwambale, a former cadet in the army, joined us at Katojo. I did not know what charges were pressed against him. As soon as he got into katojo prison, he joined other notorious inmates and started planning an escape through the roof of the prison. One night he put his plans into action. He was living in a different wing from mine. I was only able to meet him during sunshine breaks. One night we heard gunshots at the prison. I thought, we were going to be killed. This was the time Milton and his group was trying to escape through the roof; they had opened the ceiling and three of them were up in the ceiling but were discovered by the night guard before they could jump off the roof. They were brought down, beaten, stripped naked and locked in a maximum-security cell. Life became extremely difficult after these inmates, turned criminals attempted to escape. As a matter of fact this was the beginning of prison life. While out in the community as a high profile political figure you have no freedom because any time, you expect some military or cadre person to jump on you and administer mob justice against you especially if you did not agree with and support the government's "correct political line". However while in prison, you are protected by the prison authorities, in which case, you are safer though not free. So when these disgruntled cadets tried to escape, freedom in prison was denied all of us. We were not given food for two days. We were not allowed visitation and the entire prison was punished just because of the three chaps who wanted to escape. This escape was a blessing to me in disguise. *"Everything that happens in an explainable circumstance always happens for a purpose"*. God is always in situations when He wants to deliver those he loves. The prison authorities were scared of having high profile people like me and the army cadets under their protection without enough security. An order came from the provincial prison authorities that we must be transferred to the Luzira Maximum Prison in Kampala. This was still a prison but a better prison, with the international community keeping their close eye on it. As a result of this attempted escape by those disgruntled inmates, we were transferred together with them to Kampala. As I recall, after two months in Katojo, we were transferred to Luzira. We traveled in a prison lorry with one Mutoro Lunatic whom the prison authorities wanted to take to the mental hospital in Butabika. This lunatic old man made our trip to Luzira very enjoyable and humorous, as prisoners always were miserable. For instance each time we came across a trading center or a township, he could stand up and put his hands out through the lorry window, with shackle chains around his hands. He would announce in the language of that township, the reasons why he is in shackles. For example when we passed through Fort Portal town he announced: in Lutoro that; *"bantwara, nyowe omukam wa toro, Ngu Nyangire okugura ekibiriti shilling T500"* [meaning: they have taken me, the king of toro that I have refused to buy a match box at 500/-shillings]. This man knew almost all the languages of the townships we travelled along the way from Fort Portal to Kampala. In Masaka, Lukaya and Lyantonde, he could say in Luganda that:"*bantute, Nze kabaka wa toro, ngu nagenye kugula ekibiriti sh. 500/-*". In other words, he was saying that he had been arrested and now was being taken to Luzira for refusing to buy a matchbox at 500 shillings. Practically our trip was more enjoyable as a result of this lunatic man who was entertaining us. At that time the NRM government had just devalued the Uganda shilling and a matchbox was alarmingly costing 500 shillings. This was not affordable to most low-income families. Although this man was a lunatic but he was actually telling the truth about the reality of life outside our prison walls. When we arrived in Luzira, I found more former members of parliament, and former ministers who had been arrested on fictitious charges. At Luzira we learnt that it was common practice for the government to create a charge that would keep you in prison as long as possible so that you do not live among the population; unless you chose to join and support the government; then the leadership would not suspect you for political confusion. The NRM [National Resistance Movement] philosophy was a new thing; they tried to introduce it as a party in 1980 i.e. UPM [Uganda Patriotic Movement] but could not get enough support to win more than one seat. When they went to the bush to fight the government, they did not have concrete evidence that the election was not free and fair. UPC did not defeat the leader of the movement, Mr. Yoweri Museveni. He was defeated by the Democratic Party, but did not sue the Democratic Party for defeating him; instead he went to the bush complaining that the election was not free and fair because he lost. Therefore, anyone who would explain to the people clearly that the Movement did not go to the bush because election was rigged, but went to the bush to fight their way to power, would be either eliminated or imprisoned. Such people were considered [*kipingamizi*] meaning saboteur. It was generally believed that if government removed anyone who would sabotage their campaign to introduce their "ten point program", the masses would readily accept them. That way, the ten point program which they sought to introduce after Museven was sworn in would find no resistance among the population. So right away, they came with a strategy of eliminating any forms of opposition, such that when the NRM finally wanted to have elections, it would be the only political organization on the political playground. There were so many myths that surrounded the formation of the NRM leadership, for example the assertation that they went to the bush with 27 guns to fight the government would easily be defeated if it was explained clearly by a well informed political figure. The leader of the NRM was also the Minister of Defense in the UNLF government, which means he could have had more than 27 guns. But this could not be explained to the population because whoever would explain this was either locked up in Luzira or had fled into exile.

In Luzira we were treated well as political detainees. The government made it a point to present us to the courts as the law stipulated so that the International Community does not accuse them of holding us without trial. They cleverly framed charges hard enough to prove beyond a reasonable doubt on either side of the prosecution or the defense; but would keep you remanded for as long as they wished. We were allowed to eat food from our homes prepared by people of our choice; because we had several enemies including some prisoners from the Amin era who were used as cooks. This was the only way to avoid eating poisoned food as was a rumored common practice, and if you did, then your family would never know how you died. In addition, we were allowed to sleep on mattresses placed on the floor while sharing rooms with at least 4 others. We had a wing which they called the "politicians" wing. In this wing we lived with Chris Rwakasisi, Edward Rurangaranga, James Rwanyarare and Gashom Kagurusi. A few months later, we were joined by Lutakome Kayira, Dr. Henry Bwambale, Paul Muwanga, Lt. Namiti and Amon Bazira. A day after Amon Bazira arrived, we saw two Lorries of *"panda gari"* prisoners who were picked up from the streets of Gulu and Kitgum. They called them loggers because they had no case to answer. They were paraded outside the prison office, journalist were called in and Amon Bazira was taken out of the prison and photographed with these loggers from the Northern Uganda. The next Newspapers on Kampala streets carried a huge headline story that Amon Bazira had been brought into Luzira with rebels who were planning to over through the government. When we heard this news in the press we were all amazed at how the authorities could lie to the public through the press that Bazira belonged to the *"panda gari"* loggers who now were languishing in Luzira prisons. Most of these loggers were to die in this prison due to starvation and poor sleeping conditions. Every day, they were carrying out of prison at least 3 bodies and this went on for more than three weeks without anyone raising a red flag. Eventually, the news of constant dead bodies being brought out of Luzira leaked to the Red Cross. Red Cross came to visit and found the conditions very appalling. They made a strong submission to the International Community and the Government was put to task to improve the conditions of loggers whose rate of death had increased to almost five persons per day. These were human beings who were brought from northern Uganda, because the government thought they would be easy recruits for the rebel armies especially that of Alice Lakwena's "Lord Resistance Army". This was the immediate major threat to the government after the fall of Kampala. The conditions for the loggers then improved and generally for all other prisoners. It is always tough for any new government to consolidate their authority especially when they were replacing what was considered an elected and popular government. Of course, the NRM government made several mistakes, which eventually they corrected as they become comfortable with governance. In Luzira we were with many other prisoners most of whom were solders from both the defunct UPDF-Uganda People's Defense Forces, the Amin soldiers – Uganda Army, as well as some from the NRA – National resistance Army ranks who came in for discipline and/or spying purposes. One such soldier was captain Rwamukaga who had shot and killed a former Member of Parliament in Bunyoro. As well some NRA soldiers who were responsible for indiscipline in the city were remanded in Luzira prison. We freely learnt more about their bush operations as some shared with us their bush stories and atrocities without fear. While in Luzira prison they did not know if they would be charged with criminal offences or whether they would be released and retain their jobs. It was evident that we collected free "bush" information as to how Yoweri Museveni and his army operated among the civilian population of the *"famous Luwero triangle"*.

The NRM establishment was careless as to how they threw their prisoner around prison institutions. In Luzira, we found one prisoner of Pakistan citizenship, detained without charges, his name was Sajat. He told us he used to manufacture hand grenade and homemade bombs for the Kayira rebels and later for the Museven rebels. When Lutakome Kayira joined us at Luzira, he invited this Sajat fellow in his cell. We later learnt that Kayira was planning with Sajat to remotely organize rebel activities around the Rwenzori Mountains. This idea was opposed by Dr. Henry Bwambale and Amon Bazira both influential politicians from the Rewenzori mountains. Dr. Henry Bwambale was a member of the Democratic Party while Amon Bazira was a member of the Uganda Peoples' Congress party. They disagreed with Kayira about starting rebel activities from their homeland. Kayira was disappointed because he knew without the blessing of citizens from the area; a rebel movement would never succeed. I had never been so close to Kayira as this time in prison. I was able to see the three opposing politicians, Amon Bazira, Kayira and Henry Bwambale disagreeing in principle of starting a rebel movement together while they all agreed that the NRM government should be fought and removed. They did not know how this could be done since they were all in prison and had no access to freedom. Sajat was later released and deported. It is at this time that one afternoon Lutakome Kayira and Paul Muwanga were sharing a meal together on their prison veranda. I joined them together with Henry Bwambale and Amon Bazira. We discussed generally why Ugandans tend to fight and kill each other. Kayira was a Muganda and had been fighting his fellow Muganda, Paul Muwanga when he was vice President of Uganda. Kayira asked for forgiveness from Paul Muwanga. I saw a reconciled Kayira. I saw Bazira reconciling with Dr. Henry Bwambale and asking for forgiveness for what happened during the 1980 elections, where Henry Bwambale was not allowed to be nominated as Democratic candidate. As we talked further about how to reconcile Ugandans, Kayira retorted; and he was speaking in Luganda; I quote: "*Nze banage omusaja ono agenda kunzita*". Meaning "my dear, this man is going to kill me". As if this was prophetically said, a week later Kayira was released from detention and within days, he was murdered in his home in Kampala. Of course Yoweri did not kill him, but an inquiry into his death that was ordered by President Yoweri Museven has never been made public. Scotland Yard was involved in the investigations, but still we have no results. After Kayira's death, a steady stream of bad news ensued. Paul Muwanga was released from dentition and later died in his home of illness which has never been explained. Lt. Namiti fell sick and was rushed to Mulago hospital. He later died there with unexplained circumstances.

Bazira and I kept a low profile while pursuing our cases with our lawyers without letting the press know. We believed that if the press knew of our maneuvers to fight our cases through the courts, the government would keep a tough eye on us. As it was the case in many times, people were re-arrested as soon as they left the court premises. We did not wish this to happen once we got releases.

October 27, 1987 I appeared before a High Court Judge. He asked the government prosecutor to show reasonable cause why for 18 months they have not come to the High Court to prove that there was a case to answer in my so called "kidnap" case. Because the government did not have enough evidence, the High Court Judge ordered that I be released on bail and gave the government 28 days to prove that there was a case to answer.

LIFE IN LUZIRA

Life in Luzira was much better than that of Katojo where I was first kept as a maximum-security prisoner. We lived behind bars in a prison surrounded by a brick wall taller than building blocks we lived in. There was a football field as well as an arena where everyone could mix and mingle and play other indoor games. Our favorite game was scrabble. We were allowed visitation twice each week. One of my favorite hobbies while in this prison was reading, and the bible became one of my favorite books to read. I read about Kings in the bible, I read about Jesus and the forgiveness of sins. One of the things I discovered in the bible was that I had been a disobedient servant of the Lord Almighty. I discovered that God created us each for a specific purpose. And in the execution of our purposes, we ought to be pure and transparent. I began to see lots of faults in me that deserved punishment. As a young Member of Parliament, I was not transparent towards my family, my wife did not have enough time with me, I was so unfaithful, and I paid more attention to constituency issues and other people than to my family. This was not right. Each time my wife came to visit, I saw her glittering eyes like I had never seen them before. She appeared more beautiful every time I looked at her through prison bars. After three months in this prison, I was allowed by the prison authorities to visit with my family members in a private room while watched at a distance by a warder. There were so many lessons I was learning each day I remained in prison. I began to feel sorry for the sins I had committed while I was Member of Parliament. I began to see how although I was rich, but yet I was poor in Spirit. Material wealth started to wither away, because now I was at the mercy of ruthless warders while being watched over by the Almighty God. I slowly began to realize that while I was a secular servant, I was disobedient to God to fulfill the purposes for which I was created. I began to weep over my own sins as I read more and more of the Holy Bible. I literary surrendered my life to HIM and started to see things differently. I started to thank God even for allowing this to happen because I was beginning to come to terms with reality. I saw how all people deserted me. I was no longer in position to help them therefore; there was no need even for them to see me in time of distress. But God did not abandon me even one second. If Psalm 23 ever head any mean to my life, this was it.

While in Luzira, I was waiting upon the power of God to prevail. I secluded myself from other inmates one night and went into prayer by myself. It was 3:00 am on one morning when I lit a candle and moved into the cell corridors so that I do not wake up other prisoners. I did not want any prison warder to see light in our cell room while I was praying.

In that corridor, I opened my bible and read Jeremiah chapter 29:11...

When I saw what Lord told Jeremiah that He had plans for him, plans for a good future, plans for prosperity and not disaster. I prayed to the same God of Jeremiah. First I told this God that, I am not Jeremiah, but "if you Lord have plans for me, just like you had for Jeremiah, then answer my prayers". This is what I told that God in my prayer in the prison cell corridor that day: *"God, you know me by name. Even before I was born you already knew me. God even before I became the youngest Member of Parliament, you already knew me. God even before I came into this prison, you already knew, and you also know when I will get out of here. God I pray that you get me out of here quickly so that I can fulfill the purposes for which you called me. Lord I know there are many ways people get out of such prisons. They either escape, or there happens to be a coup and prisoners are released, or even better still, they go to court and are declared innocent and released. God if you can use one of these ways to get me out of here, I will work for you to fulfill the purposes for which you called me by name". I pray this in the wonderful name of Jesus Christ. Amen".* I concluded my simple prayer with a silent song of worship in the Rutoro Hymn Book number 123. I started praising the Lord and believing that freedom was a foot. It did not come right away. I spent another 4 months before I was produced before the high court judge. God chose the best way to set me free. It was not through escape, neither was it through a coup de etat. The government for which I wished the coup still rules today and may probably be there for another 10 or so years. God in his infinite wisdom reigned over my fears, led me through prison towards praise. After Luzira, I stayed in Kampala for two weeks before I moved to my hometown. I first went to the central police station to report, and there I encountered no problem at all. The good Lord was with me.

Chapter 17

THE ULTIMATE ESCAPE

December 27, 1987 was the day I made a real escape. News came to my house in Kilembe that military intelligence personnel were in town and were wondering whether a former Member of Parliament who recently got out of Luzira was still in Kampala. Their informer actually misinformed them and reported that I was not in Kampala but that I was in my home village of Kyarumba visiting parents and relatives.

The same informer hired a taxi and drove to my house in Kilembe to come and tell me of what was about to happen. He said, "Men in civilian clothes were in town on mission to pick you up and detain you in a military prison". The military prisons as we knew them were more of torture chambers than actually prison cells. People there were living a life of torment and deep suffering, which resulted in most cases death. I couldn't envisage myself getting into torture chambers after gaining my freedom from Luzira. I knew God was with me and I also knew that it was God who sent this informer to tip me of what was eminent. I did not take anything for granted. I told my wife to once again take courage and stay alone. I told her, that she had endured tough times while I was in Luzira. I did not want her to face the same yet again if I was unfortunate enough to join those in military cells. This is the place where there were reported gross abuses of human rights. These were places where Red Cross was never allowed to visit. These were places like the notorious Basima house where the International Community would never be told what was going on there. I had to elude this, by quickly stepping out and convincing my wife that God will take care of her with her two little kids, and that he would take care of me as I go into the unknown. I told her, that as long as I was alive, God will take care of us, and will reunite us to serve him. I kissed her goodbye and headed for the nearest boarder. A good friend of mine played the role of a Good Samaritan. He gave me his car; I traveled through the main road passing through roadblocks without being detected. Later at night I crossed the border into Congo, which was then called Zaire. This was the real escape. I was met at the boarder post in Zaire by a Military Colonel who was in charge of that area. At the time there were insurgents fighting to remove the government of then President Mubutu Sese Seko of Zaire. These insurgents were having hideouts in Uganda. As soon as I sat in the military helicopter, I knew that I had gotten myself out of Uganda, and that my escape had been successfully executed. The helicopter dropped me in a small town called Beni in a Military Barracks. Four days later, government agents transported me to the city of Goma where I was handed over to immigration. Asylum was processed and a United High Commissioner for Refugees' card was issued to me. I was then left to vend for myself in a town I had no clue how thing were done. I could not speak French. If I wanted to teach English, I was required to know some French or better still some Swahili. It was going to be difficult to get a job in this town, I told my self. My hotel expense account was over, I was required to pay or check out. I actually checked out and found myself under the care of the Goma CPZA church. This was a Community of Churches under the Pentecostal Assemblies of Zaire. The church pastor here inquired of me if I would be willing to wake up at 5:00am to pray with the rest of the staff. I said yes, and I knew that God answers prayers. I stayed at this church for seven days, and when I moved out, I made this my regular church. I prepared myself for a life of uncertainties. I continued to pray that God will take care of my family in Uganda, and enable them to join me. With God's help I was able to find someone who regularly traveled to Uganda, and became the link to my family.

We connected with my family and agreed that we reunite and live together though in a foreign land. We would seek God's guidance for the next move. My wife moved into Zaire living behind a country she served as a Teacher and Young Women's Christian Association Outreach Worker. She came to a country where she neither knew the official language, French nor the local language Swahili. She depended on her capacity to learn and adapt. Strong willed as she was, she started what were to become the worst days of her life. She had lost her status as a wife of a former Member of Parliament, she had lost her civil life as a teacher and now she would be subjected to a village life, full of suffering, and uncertainties. With the little money she came with from our country, we were able to rent one small town house for one year. We were able to save some money for food on a regular basis. We could not afford to put our son in preschool. We joined a prayer group headed by a lady – Mama Feza, who not only was a parent, but she became a Spiritual mother. She prayed for us, and gave prophesies about what God had in store for us if we could only trust in Him. She was an encouraging spiritual leader and we enjoyed being part of her prayer group. Amon Bazira who had been released in early January 1988 joined us in Goma. We did not immediately know the circumstances under which he left the country. He joined us in the prayer group and at one time we agreed with each other that if we should ever go back to Uganda, a prayer group like this one, where people came for healing, restoration and salvation should be introduced in our communities. **Prayer centers** where people came to seek the living God was what was lacking in Uganda. The country had become morally corrupt and needed God even through the leadership. Our money was running out and life was increasingly becoming tough to manage. We decided to leave Goma immediately and migrate to Beni where we could be close to relatives and friends. Amon Bazira on his part moved to Kinshasa and was being looked after by the Mubuto government. In Beni, we spoke the same language. After we moved into Beni, a movement called NALU headed by Amon Bazira was formed. There were disturbances along the Zaire and Uganda boarders. As we got more squeezed with hunger and no money, we were contemplating going back to our land and face the real tortures in the military; but God said no. There was confusion in Uganda about the existence of rebels along the boarder. In fact there were no rebels as such. The name NALU was so scary that people thought Amon Bazira had mercenaries and that the Zairian army was backing him. This was a total misrepresentation of the situation. NALU was just a myth at this time. There was to be no war, as Amon and Henry had prevented Kayira from staging rebel activities along the Rwenzori Mountains. Bazira was not about to make the same mistake. But it was common knowledge that war was imminent and when army officers from the government defected into Congo so that they could join the *"imaginary NALU"* army, they were unceremoniously disappointed because they had believed a pack of lies about the existence of an army with mercenaries that was ready to remove Museven from power. These lies about the existence of an army called NALU actually motivated Bazira to seek help from Mubutu and Arap Moi to fight against the National Resistance Movement. Bazira did not live to see this army in action as he died in 1993 and thereafter that army that was still a myth vanished. Museven still rules today and there have been chunks of such lies over the years beginning from Lakwena in the North, to Peter Otai in the East and to Itongwa in the Central as well as Tubliqs ADF in the West. There was the "Kirimutu group" in Bunganda for which Dr. Henry had been implicated and detained. There is still the "Lord Resistance Army" in the North that has caused untold suffering to the people of Acholi land. All these groups have come and gone living the civilian population in turmoil. People have had breaking hearts, absolutely dominated by sadness and deep frustrations as they continue to see their children get abducted and forced to join useless armies in a bid to oust the sitting government. It has not worked and may not work in years to come. The days of rebel activities expired in the 1986 and now we have democratic practices remaining to be the basis for removing a government. In Acholi land, we have heard of untold suffering by children who walk day and night looking for safe havens. They have nicknamed them "night commuters". This did not happen before the double Okellos ignored democratic practice to remove a government. A group of eight army personnel deserted the NRM to join Amon Bazira's NALU Army. They were held at the border because even Bazira was not aware of their coming. These defectors were kept at the border town while the authorities in Beni were awaiting instructions from Kinshasa, the capital of Congo. The Ugandan deserters were told to hold on here until word came from Kinshasa to decide their fate. They had wanted to climb the mountains to hide in the forest until Amon Bazira came. I told Major Kapuchu and Major Patrick Muhindo that if they had come to join Bazira's Army, there was none and that they were "now the army". I told them that going to the mountains would be futile for the people of Kasese where they came from. Amon himself had not invited them because he had nothing on the ground to warrant fighting a government, which was increasingly becoming popular with the people. Bazira had other plans as he had shared with me, plans of using conventional war that would exclude the population of Kasese. He was working with Kenya, Sudan and Zaire to explore a conventional method which would demobilize Kampala without affecting Kasese. Meanwhile, I had wanted to travel to Kinshasa, and had failed to get enough money to buy a ticket. I believed in my heart that if God allowed me to get out of luzira, he would enable me to reach Kinshasa where I could be able to speak English because this was a capital city where embassies were located and most of the people there spoke some English. I hoped to look for employment in the capital while seeking to move out of the country for resettlement.

An opportunity came knocking on my door for me to travel to the capital with the defectors. An order had come from the Military in Kinshasa that the fugitives from Uganda should not be allowed to live by the boarder as they were intending to stage military operations against a neighboring country. I did not know that they were under arrest. They had crossed the border illegally. But the good news for them was that Uganda and Congo did not have extradition treaty. Although they were under arrest, they would not be deported. They were to be moved away from the boarder so that they do not cause bitterness and suffering along the common border. I was requested by the 'commission de zone' of this local town to accompany this team to the capital to help explain why they crossed the border in the manner in which they came. Why the Commission de zone chose me, I did not have a clue, but God did and I grabbed the opportunity and accepted the offer. I was to travel to the capital, on *a free ticket* in an army transport plane. What a blessing, I thought to myself. This had been my dream and I had almost lost faith in prayer. My wife did not lose faith though for she continued to intercede on behalf of the entire family.

It was now time for us to board the plane to Kinshasa. The instructions were that they were picking up eight fugitives but the commissioner de zone presented nine people. They did not appear to be bothered by the extra person. The pilot just shrugged his shoulders. I was happy that they did not insist on leaving me behind. We happily jumped into the military transport plane a C130. After a five hours flight, we landed in a military airport called Ndolo. A prisons truck was waiting with instruction to pick up eight [8] Ugandan fugitives but was dismayed to see nine. They had no choice but to take all the nine. I was number 9 and was not a fugitive, but they had to take me with them anyways. It was at this point that we realized that we were getting into a military jail. The unpredictable reality had again kicked in. We headed for a short but painful jail term. Freedom was again snatched and this time in a foreign land.

Chapter 18

FROM FREEDOM TO PRISON – SECOND EPISODE.

The Democratic Republic of Congo is a vast country with close to zero communication networks. At the time we lived there between 1987 and 1992 it was called Zaire, led by the notorious dictator Mubutu Sese Seko Kuku Gwendu wa Zabanga. He was a close friend of Idi Amin. He and his MPR leaders had amassed great wealth abroad, which left the country empty of social infrastructure. Mubutu had been the darling of the West since he took over power from the Belgians. Belgium's king Leopold had treated Congo as his personal business property. As long as Mubutu promised the Western imperialists, that he would prevent communism from setting foot on the African soil, his gross violation of human rights was ignored. He committed many crimes against his own people, including denying them the basic rights to civilization and basic infrastructure. At least by the time we lived in Congo [Zaire] there was no road that would lead you from one city in the West to another in the East. For example, you could only fly from Goma in order to get to Kinshasa. To get to Kisangani from Goma by road you needed at least one to two weeks of truck driving. The few existing roads were horribly dilapidated with deep potholes and overgrown bushes.

When we arrived in Kinshasa it appeared as if we had entered another country altogether. We saw a city, with a population of more than 6 million people with trenches of water uncared for. This is one of the African cities with sky scrapers and roads with overpasses, and with an unfinished monument structure which might never be completed. Mubutu was a *'small lord'* on the African soil. He controlled other leaders such as Habyaliman of Rwanda and Buyoya of Burundi. They were like his classroom monitors while he was the Head Prefect. But once communism crumbled, taking Mubutu's usefulness with it, his external support from America and Europe evaporated. Military vehicles and aircrafts crowded the military airport where we landed. We entered his country during his last days when his grip on power both in his country and his controlled neigbouring countries was slipping. Wide spread anarchy was the order of the day. His own military gurus were denuding the country left and right, and discontent in the army was prevalent. We could feel it as we arrived in the capital city of Kinshasa. Widespread demonstrations were evidenced in streets and at the University of Kinshasa. We were ordered to move two by two into a prisons truck. One of the fugitives, Major Muhindo tried to resist. He told the military officer on site that, I quote; "we are military personnel from Uganda, and we should not be under arrest". The man clearly responded in Lingala language, quote; "*yo. Kanga munoko nayo, awa ezali Uganda tee*" meaning, "you shut up your probosis, this is not Uganda." At this point I knew for sure that we had been denied our freedom and we were going to be confined to yet another prison, this time in a foreign land. I did not know what to expect. We were driven for about 30 minutes into a military prison. In this prison we found military officers who had been locked up for indiscipline and others with various crimes ranging from corruption to treason. They had access to television news, and were allowed newspapers. They slept on beds like school dormitories, and eat food from their homes. One of us lamented, "this is not bad". While in this prison, we were informed by the military officer in charge that we were ordered to come here because Uganda was seeking the extradition of the eight fugitive soldiers. We even saw on National television Ugandan President Museven meeting with his Zairian host President Mubutu at his Gbadolite resort home, the equivalent of *'rwakitura'*. At the meeting they discussed bilateral issues such as boarder security, trade, refuges, and behind closed doors we were told, that Mubutu told Museven emphatically that he could not hand over any refugees who seek asylum in his country. We were told that it is at this meeting that Museven developed deep hatred for Mubutu and vowed to assist anyone who would overthrow him. Museven did not trust Mubutu and he now knew that his boarder on the west would never be secure as long as Mubutu was in control in Kinshasa. Mubutu's downfall started after this meeting as Laurent Kabila's ragtag rebels who were scatted all over East Africa started to "swallow their saliva". [An African saying when excitement of success starts to emerge.] It would not be too long before Yoweri Museven gave Laurent Kabila full support to erase the dictator from the face of the planet and drive Congo into deeper turmoil as they plunder the leftovers. The support of Kabila by Yoweri Museven did not only culminate in a security measure along the common boarder; it exposed a commercial enterprise by both Uganda and Rwanda, so ruthless in its design and so pitiless in its implementation that resulted in the extermination of millions of people in the North and South Kivu Provinces. It became a scramble for wealth by both Ugandan and Rwandese armies. Under the disguise of securing common boarders of Uganda and Rwanda, and riding them of rebels and bandits, Uganda and Rwandan soldiers amassed tremendous wealth from Congo's timber, gold, diamonds, and other precious minerals. It is unfortunate that the United States and United Nations turned a blind eye as they did in 1994 when Rwandese were busy massacring each other in what has come to be known as the worst genocide of modern times. People speaking the same language and with the same culture decimated each other to almost one million people; just because some were Tustsi and others were Hutu both struggling for political power.

Once Mubutu Sese Seku died in 1997, his giant country seemed to have died with him as was described by Madeleine Drohan in her book, "Making a Killing". She contends, "The foreign armies were not the only vultures feeding off the corpse of the Congo. They worked alongside and sometimes in concert with criminal groups, arms traffickers, diamond smugglers, rebel groups' and companies that saw the potential for profit in a conflict zone."[Drohan 291].

When President Museven had long returned to Kampala after his last visit to Gbadolite, Amon Bazira was arrested in Rwanda by the Habyalimana government. They wanted to trade him for their own fugitives who were in Uganda. Hyabyalimana and Mubutu were great friends. When Mubutu's security staff in Goma heard that a Uganda high profile rebel leader was being held in Kigali, they hurriedly went to rescue him and rushed him to Kinshasa. A district delegation left Kasese to demand that Bazira be arrested and handed over to Uganda because he was going to cause trouble at the boarder by starting a movement which would threaten the stability of Uganda. This delegation was headed by then District RC5. They met with their counter parts in Beni, and were told that Kinshasa had arrested the fugitives and their leader and all would be handed over. They were deceived! They went back to Bwera with what they considered good news and held rallies at Mpodwe and Kasese claiming that Bazira was going to be handed over to them. There were jubilations all over the district with Members of Parliament and other local leaders celebrating what later became a hoax. They had been lied to, as this backfired with embrassement. Bazira was at loose, and indeed he became a pain in the neck of the Ugandan government. It was common knowledge that if he started a movement, he would attract a huge number of following. As he was trotting between Kinshasa, Khartoum and Nairobi, the long arm of NRM security operatives caught up with him and in 1993 his body was found on one of Kenya's highway. An inquiry into his death by the Kenya government has never been ordered and we may never know the circumstance under which he died. The Kasese population for whom he served as Member of Parliament still misses him.

Three weeks later, we were transferred from the military prison to a worse detention centre. The special intelligence unit called A.N.D- [Agence Nationale de Defance] manned this. In this place we were treated like real criminals, we were not given regular meals, we were not allowed to take regular baths and we were only allowed out on the sunshine once a day for only one hour. We were fed one meal a day, that amount to nothing as the quantity was small and the quality was extremely poor. Our freedom was taken away. We were told we mounted to nothing because we came from a country that had haboured insurgents for many years fighting against the government of President Mobutu. After spending three weeks of untold suffering in prison, we were visited by a group of Red Cross officials. They spoke to us one by one. When they came to me, I showed them my identifications, and they wondered why I was in this prison with this group. They immediately contacted the United Nations High Commissioner for Refugees to inform them that a conventional refugee was being held with Ugandan army deserters.

The next day, they came back with a staff from the United High Commissioner to rescue me. The Red Cross pleaded for the other eight fugitives to be rescued as well. We were all released from this dungeon and handed over to the UNHCR.

In the mean time, upcountry my wife who appeared abandoned and frustrated was having the greatest share of shame and suffering. She was lonely and living a life of scorn even by kids. She was trying to unload the double and often multiple yoke on her back as she was taking care of two little people. She was living with strangers who finally became to be family thereafter. Through her religious medium of prayer, she called out for help. In her own solitary confinement in a room of prayer, she often yelled to an invisible God and the scorn came from the neigbours and children as to when that invisible God would hear her cry. Like the average rural woman she had become, whose dilemma she often internalized, she calls for spiritual help to balance her load like her rural counter parts; that had become part of her life in the prayer group. These rural women had become like her traditional sisters. This relationship was to last into an everlasting friendship and sisterhood. Apart from being domestically discouraged, she did not lose the spirit of trusting in the invisible living God, who ultimately answered her call for help in the long run. While for the four years she lived without my intimate relationship, she was almost fully integrated into the African rural culture although she lived with the stigma in the periphery of the high social class which she had just been ejected out of, a high table social class of *"women of status."*

In Kinshasa, the UNHCR settled us into a transitional house in one of the busy neigbourhoods of the city. We were free at last.

As we lingered around the capital, free at last, we saw opportunities for resettlement knock on our doors. There was a glimpse of hope. As I visited various embassies and High Commissions in Kinshasa, I came to know how people got resettled in other countries. I spoke to the eight deserters that we needed to find a way out of this congested massive city. Everyone in the group had different ambitions. It is at this point that I realized God had sent them across the border not to come and cause trouble, but to air lift me from the rural life of suffering to the city life of opportunities and hope. God indeed created a way, where there was no way. As for them, one by one they returned to Uganda through various ways. They refused my idea of seeking resettlement to another country. Some of them actually fulfilled their desire to go into the bush to fight but when they realized that the bush was a wise option, they surrendered. Others simply went straight back to Uganda. It is here that we concluded that there was a *divine* push for them to cross the border. They did not know that the actual motive was *not for them to come down to wage war* against their country. *God did it as HE always has the last move*. It was all spiritually motivated. God had a purpose for our lives, and the work he had started in us, had to be accomplished through us, by Him. Phil.1: 6. The good work of initiating schools to enhance literacy in the Ruwenzori had to be finished. And as it says, in John 15:16 that, "we did not chose him, but he chose us, to bear fruit, fruit that will last for generations to enjoy" [paraphrased NIV]. A way had to be found in which our lives could be preserved so that our works would glorify His name.

As the group of defectors left Congo [Zaire], I used my crudely earned freedom to continuously visit various embassies in the capital to pressurize for resettlement. I forgot for a little while that I had a family far away up country although I knew for a fact that even if I did remember, there was no way I could get in touch with them. It was like I was in another exile, and I felt sorry for my wife who continued to endure the pressure of shame by herself without me at her side. I also forgot for a little while that I had prayed in **Luzira Prison** for God to grant me freedom in order to work for Him. Sounds familiar? We all forget so quickly. The UNHCR was not willing to find a place for me in a third country. They urged that my life was not in any danger. However, I ignored them and moved around to check with various other embassies. The British Embassy in Kinshasa was my immediate target and my turning point.

I spoke to the Immigration Counselor named Schneider [*not real name*]. I had received this reference from my long old friend Tom Stacey from UK who had advised me to talk to Mr. Schneider and asked about the possibility of migrating to the UK. I was told that Britain was more sympathetic to the Museven' government, therefore they would not be accepting people running away from Uganda. They considered Uganda safe for all people to live. [the usual diplomatic language]. They did not get my point. I nonetheless was able to convince him that Uganda was not suitable for me at this point after narrating all that had happened to me. All he did was to give me his business card and asked me to give it to the Protection Officer at the UNHCR office in Kinshasa. He wanted the protection office to call him so that they discuss options for me to get out of the Congo. The Protection Officer after seeing that I had moved beyond their diplomatic sphere of influence, he did not call him. He simply gave me application forms and assured me that they will find a country for me. Within days, I was scheduled to attend three interviews; Canada, USA and Australia. I attended the Canadian interview first, and at the end of the interview, the immigration officer who had traveled from Abidjan, Ivory Coast, told me: "congratulations, you have passed the interview and will be resettled into Canada". He requested for my family to be brought from the upcountry of Congo Beni zone to be precise, into the capital to join me as we prepare to travel to the country of the Maple Leaf, Canada. The UNHCR made immediate arrangements to bring my family. They prepared air tickets for all my family including the 7 year old son who was left in Uganda.

My wife who had felt abandoned for a while, but not by God, finally reunited with me and we were a complete family again. We went through the immigration procedures of the Canadian embassy, a process that took almost two year. In this waiting process, we were able to add a fourth child to conclude our number of six. At the time of departure, we received a test of faith. God sent one friend of ours to bid us farewell and delivered to us five [5] US dollars to come with to Canada. This friend had his son in the United States and wanted me to buy stamps to mail a letter to his son. We did not know that 5 dollars was a blessing that would carry us into the unknown and prosper us to turn our eyes to God and listen to what He had destined us to do. The works God started in us even before we knew Him intimately had to be accomplished. We had just started. More lay ahead, dealing with people's attitudes, the spirit of reconciliation among the entire people referred to in this reading. Forgiveness and building strong bridges. The traumatic situations and conditions our whole family was subjected to during this whole journey could not be ignored. God prepared us to travel this far to examine with other immigrants, different aspects of life. God planned this journey to use our experiences to help others in similar traumatic circumstances.

Chapter 19

THE UNDENIABLE GOD GIVEN "Ts"

God, the Lord of creation endowed each one of us with Time, Talents and Treasures. We all have various beliefs which make us live one day at a time. As for me I am convinced that God created me with a set of talents, gave me time that He alone only knows how much of it I will live to enjoy, as well he gave me Treasures that totally belong to Him; but I must manage them. As a Manager of God's treasures, He gave us time and we have to use the talents to make good of God's expectations. This is true for almost all human beings. I was blessed with a wonderful wife with tremendous talents so that we would be able to exercise our creativity as a team to accomplish what has been entrusted to us in the form of the three T's before we hit eternity. At the time of writing this book, majority of our time has been lived in North America and we still have a debt to account for the time and treasures we have been entrusted with. As mentioned earlier we arrived in North America with five [$5] United States dollars as our treasure to start a life. As soon as we settled in, we were amazed at how much emphasis was placed on time. We came to learn immediately that Time was money; therefore, treasure was attached to Time. Since we have lived majority of our time here, we have come to learn to do all things as regulated by time. The God given time now has to be managed according to the North American standards. Regular work is paid for according to how much time an employee has put into as production is measured and determined by time. It is common knowledge that time is of essence for every one under the sun, therefore we have to be diligent enough to be accountable on earth before we are called to account someday in eternity. We have got talent and time to manage, therefore Edith Kambere and I decided to put our talent together to form an organization which we called Umoja Operation Compassion Society. 'Umoja' because we combined our time and talent together to serve people as one. 'Operation' because we had to act in good faith while voluntarily using our treasures and 'compassion' because we had been treated with compassion in foreign lands as we traveled to our current destination. We thought we had to treat others with compassion since our heavenly father was "full of compassion, slow to anger and rich in love". [Ps 145:8] as he took us to places we did not know we would reach.

As we invested our time, talent and treasure into this organization, we saw tremendous growth among the people we targeted to serve; the new immigrants.

We devoted our time outside of our regular work schedule into helping new arrivals from Africa to integrate well into Canadian communities. We opened our home to strangers who came from Africa without discriminating which country they came from at no cost. As the Organization started to grow, we registered it into a Charitable Organization and saw a huge influx of people from Sudan, Liberia, Sierra Leone, Congo, Somalia and Burundi coming through the doors of the registered Umoja charity. Most of the people we encountered left their countries of origin as a result of being displaced by either famine as a natural disaster or the perils of war. War as we know it, is not nice. War is never a welcome encounter. George Orwell in his book 1984 says; "War is peace, freedom is slavery and ignorance is strength". [p29]. He was predicting the future where Eurasia would be at war with Eastasia and Oceania would come in as mediator to bring peace. The future is now, where rumors of war looms everywhere, bodies lie on city streets and a steady stream of bad news looms all over most of the third and developing world alike. This century's wars cannot be interpreted in terms of peace according to George Orwell.

The first and second world wars were fought to liberate the world of dictators like Hitler of Germany who had wanted to dominate the whole world. Massive migration occurred as a result of these wars. However, Orwell contends in Nineteen Eighty-Four book that "*war, it will be seen, is now a purely internal affair. In the past the ruling groups of all countries although they might recognize their common interest and therefore limit the destructiveness of war, did fight against one another, and the victor always plundered the vanquished. In our own day they are not fighting against one another at all.* **The war is waged by each ruling group against its own subjects**, *and the object of the war is not to make or prevent conquest of territory, but to keep the structure of society intact.*" [P 207]. This is exactly why third world dictators stick to power to maintain their status quo; they suppress opposition and there causing war from within.

In his book, A terrible love of War, James Hillman contends that, "war is first of all a psychological task because it threatens your life and mine directly and the existence of all living things". It therefore goes without a shadow of a doubt that war and peace are not related and cannot co-exist. African leaders who have been branded as lovers of war, or war mongers should be directed towards a peaceful exit, in order to set their people free.

Karl Marx and Aristotle's struggles of classes and logic of opposites respectively were based on the notion that war determines our thought patterns. These two philosophers determined that, "we think in war terms, feel ourselves at war with ourselves, and unknowingly believe predation. Territorial defense, conquest and the interminable battle of opposing forces are the ground rules of existence". [James Hillman]. But the questions are, are these the real ground rules of existence in today's culture? The world today especially the developing and the third world tend to groom up leaders who are inclined to the usual contemplation of conflict, where war has not been fully examined seriously, and merely relegate to mire military history; as the study of war by scholars and reporters has taken a back seat and has been isolated in policy institutions of the main stream – the West. In Africa, as most countries gained their independences, the endless wars, body counts and bloodshed have been the characteristics of post independence era. The effects of wars since the Second World War have started to show up in the baby boomers who are now the current leaders on the African continent. Since their independences, most African leaders have steered their countries through the highway to disaster by fanning the never ending wars in their nations. The effects of these wars are psychological and traumatizing. Therefore, at the start of our new society with compassionate values we had to recognize these as a matter of fact. As new immigrants arrive in any new country, they come carrying with them the effects of war, which must be dealt with immediately before they integrate into their new communities. Our work with these newcomers regardless of where they came from earned me the prestigious VanDusen award of community leadership awarded by the United Way of the Lower mainland in 2008. *"The W.J. VanDusen Community Service Award recognizes an individual for remarkable commitment and dedication to volunteerism. Award nominations are open to United Way funded organizations. The award was presented in June at United Way's Annual Leadership Reception hosted by the University of British Columbia."*

At my acceptance speech, I made several observations, but among them, one particular statement stood out. "When we arrive, there is the 'we' that society does not see: Our rich cultural values, our spiritual values, our unwavering faiths, plus our traumatic conditions that we arrive with.

Many of the immigrants who came from war-ravaged areas came having witnessed horrible situations, children see houses set on fire, see their parents arrested or beaten or raped, and then as they arrive here, we do not see the "real them." [umoja website]. These are fundamental issues newcomers from war stricken nations come with. The systems then start the stereotype game of branding them with the evils of the "... *isms*". These issues compelled us to start a literacy program for newcomers which ties in with the celebrating of literacy in Africa, especially the Rwenzori region of western Uganda, to which most of the work in this book is directed. The numerous people we have seen coming from Sudan, Sierra Leone, Congo, Somalia confirmed to us that effects of wars can lead to mental health issues which are often difficult to identify on arrival in a new country. The level of illiteracy among all new immigrants was extremely high as we came to discover. With every 10 new immigrants served at umoja, 6 were illiterate in their own language; this means they could neither read nor write in their native language. These language barriers are not readily identified by the main stream service providers since these new immigrants dive into isolation as they are engulfed by the infamous cultural shock on arrival. One of the strategies we employed to help them, was to enable them realize that in a new country they need to develop friendships that can ultimately be deep, purposeful and transformational. These would make a difference in how they would live their lives in a new environment. We had to impress upon those we interacted with; that socializing in the "western culture" was radically different from the way it is done in the "third world". It is important that as we settle in a new culture, preservation of our heritage would help in setting the stage to be transformed through affirmation, mutual support of those we came with and provide the unconditional love while impressing the new culture. Emphasis was placed on the need to preserve and consider their God given cultural heritage and ancestry and to add accountability and genuine encouragement and support. In so doing they would have created for themselves friendships that will assist them to excel in all areas of their new life. The Umoja Operation Compassion that we formed was to be a medium of passing on these qualities and values to new immigrants and would as well be responsible for informing immigrants that they have come to a culture with a lifestyle where popular media clouds the picture of popular culture. It is common general knowledge that television, movies, and numerous aggressive commercials do not offer particularly accurate portrayal of the real life. The real life of a newcomer would first be realized as they come out of isolation. The notion of culture shock drives them into isolation and for them to come to terms with real life; they would need to be self sufficient. This would be a key principle in the strategy employed by Umoja Operation Compassion in delivering the services geared to the principle of "arrive, survive and thrive".

Umoja has served as a conduit for clientele from more than 10 countries ranging from Africa as well as Afghanistan, Burma, Iran, Iraq and Jamaica. It is the never ending wars and lack of democracy that is causing all havoc with new immigrants. Take for example, "an election is stolen before it even began" in Haiti. [Globe and Mail Nov. 29]. Thousands took to the streets to protest the polls and plunged the whole country into a political crisis. As governments interfere with political processes to rig elections in their favour, the citizens are left with no choice but to move into war. First internal displacement occurs, then massive migration into neigbouring countries; a formation of refugee camps.

Life in refugee camps is extremely unbearable. Camps are often crowded with children, families and camp staff. The conditions are deplorable, sanitation is below acceptable standard, and immoral behavior is sometimes the order of the day. Internally displaced people sometimes face much more hardships than those living in protected United Nation High Commission for Refugee camps. In Northern Uganda for example, where the Lord Resistance rebel group terrorized the population for many years, civilians were hauled into Internally Displaced camps. Those camps were sometimes raided by the rebel army or sometimes by bandits, breakaway from the government army. The children who are usually the easy victims trekked long nights in search of safety in the city. They were referred to as "night commuters" since they were commuting at night to the city and during the day they would commute back to the village to stay in the camps. These children along with their parents lived a life of torture, torment and if they found a chance to sneak out of the camps into neigbouring country, they would end up in real refugee camps. If they were lucky enough to be selected for resettlement, they would end up either in North America, Australia, or New Zealand. They would come with a concealed inner torment that would be detrimental to their mental health and if they remained in isolation, they would probably develop mental illness and become dysfunctional members of society. All this because of useless wars fought by people wanting to gain access to state power so that they join the corruption circuit of undemocratic leaders. In my advocacy meetings, I have often urged that these people in refugee camps often do not choose to come to either North America or Australia. They are selected by the resettlement staff, interviewed and depending on the danger they face either in the camp or in the home country, they are offered resettlement. If their villages were safe of war, they would have preferred to be repatriated back to their home villages.

But because war still rages on, they accepted to leave the horrible life in the camp and come to civilized places with formal structures of living. They deserve to be assisted by the host country as they are coming to be part of the contributing tax payers. Settlement agencies shoulder the burden of helping these newcomers integrate well in their new communities. But the lack of funding from either the Federal Government or the Provincial Government prevents them from carrying out the burden in an effective manner. These agencies, like Umoja, depend on proposals and grant requests to carry out this noble task of helping newcomer immigrants and refugees.

Chapter 20

FORMATION OF PARTNERSHIPS

Formation of partnerships in North America is a key factor in developing non profits organizations. While Umoja was operating in a house basement, there was need to form partnerships in order to run programs. The first group we dealt with was the *Kla-how-eya Aboriginal Centre*, a not for profit organization that supports the aboriginal people in the city of surrey. This organization allowed Umoja to conduct workshops under their roof without paying any rent. We were directed to this centre by the Make Children First coalition. The City of Surrey with their Parks and Recreations provided a wonderful partnership to work with. One of the factors which helped umoja to excel was the constant attendance of meetings with the Make Children First group which focused on families with young children. The investment in the lives of children was cherished by the Make Children First table who lobbied the provincial government for funding. With strong connections with the United Way of the Lower Mainland, funds which were left over from Success by Six program at the make children first were allocated to umoja to enable us start a similar program among the African immigrants. Due to cultural shock, African immigrants were living in isolation and needed a society like ours to transition them into main stream service providers. Many of them were finding surviving difficult and would never thrive if they remain in isolation. This became the beginning of a steady support from the United Way. All the funding we received from both the United Way and Vancouver Foundation had to be spent on programs supporting immigrants in the lower mainland. We had to hire staff to run these programs such as literacy, sewing, parent and outreach programs. We did not know how far God would stretch us to fulfill His purpose. The immigrants who came to North America left a world behind which was hurting in terms of literacy, poverty and disease. The mission of Umoja is "*To empower immigrants and other newcomers to integrate into Canadian society; and to support initiatives to improve the quality of life in Africa.*" This mission would help us fulfill our vision which is "to build stronger communities, moving from newcomers to neighbours"

The part of improving the quality of life in Africa was the next issue we need to embark on. Abject poverty, disease and illiteracy were rampant among African villages. This is exemplified by the immigrants who came to Canada from refugee camps. This poverty and illiteracy had to be addressed in a more pragmatic way. We did not want to wait for large organizations like CIDA to continue spending their resources using the governments who, due to corruption did not serve the people for whom the aid was intended. Through the bureaucracy probably only about 10% of the total Aid reach its final destinations. In this 21st Century, people still lack clean water. Health centers still lack medication, even with universal education, 75% of elementary students still cannot read and write. In order to deal with this illiteracy, Umoja decided to open a learning institution in the Village of Rwentutu. The first partners who allowed their donations to be used outside Canada were from the Broadway church. The church had a Missions Committee which directed mission funds to the needy in African and elsewhere in the third world. We negotiated with the Church's Mission Committee to converse volunteers who would go to Rwentutu to break ground for the first classrooms.

In 2006 **Edith Kambere** [centre] led a team to Kasese, to lay the foundation for a school we had wanted to start in 1986. This was exactly 20 years after God had put a stop to what was going to be a school built out of frustration and political anger. The people of Rwentutu village embraced the idea of a school for their kids starting from K – 7. A Committee of Parents to oversee the planning of the school was formed. People in Uganda are not used to the idea of volunteering. We had to negotiate with the local people so as to get some manpower to assist in the construction of the first classroom block. We received help from the Pacific Academy of Surrey in addition to Broadway church. I was determined to look for more partnerships in order to have enough support to warrant starting a school abroad. With tremendous support I received from the churches and other Christian institutions such as pacific academy and Classrooms for Africa, we agreed to start a Christian school offering Christian education while embracing the Ugandan national curriculum in a private school setting.

In 2007, the parents requested that the school should simply start even though the classroom blocks were not completed. We agreed and immediately word went out in the community that a school would be opened at Rwentutu, 90 kids were ready to start the new venture. Uganda has a Universal Free Public Education, but on the mention of a new private school, 90 kids showed up, who would otherwise not be going to school despite universal free education.

A team of 3 volunteers, Nicole, Janice and Brandon agreed to travel to Rwentutu to spend three months setting up the administration of the school as well as helping find qualified Ugandan teachers who would be pioneers of the teaching staff. Spending three months at the village created confidence among the Missions Committee that Rwentutu was safe and as such many more volunteers developed interest to go and help the needy kids of the village. Umoja became the conduit for individual donations in collaboration with some churches. St. Mark Lutheran church provided the original scholastic materials to compliment that which was purchased in Uganda to help the school. By the end of 2007, at least three teams had visited the school; among them were two teachers from the New Westminster School Board. These teachers convinced other teachers, so that on their second trip, they set up a library and equipped it with over 600 children books. The support by these teachers especially from Herbert Spencer Elementary School created confidence among potential volunteers. The friend ship that has developed between Rwentutu village kids and New Westminster kids will go a long way in enhancing literacy among the youth. Herbert Spencer elementary school staff decided to adopt Rwentutu as a sister school overseas. Children were encouraged to pair with overseas students in order to exchange letters and stories. This was one tool used to expand literacy skills to Rwentutu kids through letter writing. It also became a simple way of educating young Canadian kids of the need to help fellow young people almost half a world away from home. As well, friendship through writing and international communication allows two worlds to remain connected through education. With 56 kids sleeping at the school site, there was need for us to construct a dorm block which would separate boys from girls. The teachers from Herbert Spencer who pioneered as volunteers from Canada got involved in fundraising activities which raised funds to support the school administration and teacher development. The School was only supported financially by donations for two years. It has since become self sustaining.

THE MICRO FINANCE SUCCESS STORY:

As the village supported the school, some mothers expressed fears that their kids would not be allowed to attend school as they would not afford the nominal fee that was levied to help pay the teachers. Umoja Operation Compassion heard the call and raised only $1000 to support a Micro Finance group. 10 women registered in this program by accessing $100 from the school. This money was to help them set up small businesses so that they get money to pay for their kids' upkeep at the school. They were told to bring their excess profit back to the school so that one other woman could join the group every after three months. Within 2 years, the group grew to 16 women and by the end of 2010 the Micro Finance group had grown to 37 very successful women. Their way of living improved, some constructed brick houses and others had corrugated iron sheets as roofs for their houses. The general well-being of these families improved on top of their kids going to school. We endevoured to alleviate and improve the quality of life for these families as well as providing an education for their kids. Besides helping 37 families, Rwentutu Christian School hired 10 qualified teachers who would otherwise be unemployed. Umoja's Board Chairperson Dr. Gillian Creese visited Rwentutu to find out about the successes of the women's group. Accompanied by Edith, they interview 13 women who are part of the Micro-Finance program and heard first-hand how the ability to borrow even a small sum of money (equivalent to $60) was changing their lives and the ability to provide for their families. The women interviewed run a variety of businesses, including stores that sell a large variety of dry goods and household items, a seamstress/sewing instructor, a small restaurant owner, those trading essential food stuffs and produce (particularly cooking oil, cassava flour, tomatoes, ground nuts and salt), and those raising livestock such as pigs, goats and chickens. All of the women and their families have experienced an increased standard of living as a result of these businesses. Some were able to build better homes out of brick with tin roofs (instead of mud with thatched roofs), many can now afford school fees for their children, and everyone was better able to provide adequate food and other essentials for their families. Many of the women also experienced increased status and influence within their families and the village, were learning literacy skills for the first time, and had new hopes particularly for their daughters who were now in school.

Clean water came to the school as well as the village. A medical center was built for the benefit of the school as well as helping the community. The AIDS pandemic has been reduced due to awareness and we hope that a medical facility within the school structure will help introduce health education and outreach to the community. If Umoja Operation Compassion can make an impact with one thousand dollars, why should the population remain in poverty and misery when AID money which supplements government efforts is continuously pouring in these third world countries. There is therefore dire need to improve education as primary education is only the first step in breaking the cycle of povery, backwardness and illiteracy.

To be efficient, it is necessary to be able to learn from the past, which means having a fairly accurate idea of what happened in the past. Therefore, I have written this biographical and factual truth as a subject of my own narrative, witnesses to and participants in my own experience, and in no way coincidentally in the experiences of those with whom I have come in contact. I have wished that people do not read imaginative literature either by us or about us from a stand point of view of fiction. You need to hear the true story. And you have to read it from the one who lived it. **Lest you forget**

Chapter 21

OBUSINGA BWA RWENZURURU (RWENZURURU KINGDOM)
AFTER RECOGNITION

It has been 10 years since the obusinga Bwa Rwenzuru was recognized. In this chapter I will attempt to discuss events that have engulfed the kingdom, scandals that have led to stagnation in development or lack of it, and the ultimate betrayal in the palace that led to bloodshed and incarceration of the king and many of his followers. The reader will understand that as the kingdom was recognized, the king who had lived in the United States of America for almost 30 years was coming to reign over a people that had chronically been invested with contagious partisan views as well as initiating a new kingdom administration with no resources at all and frankly facing modern day institutional management challenges of which he had no mental capacity to handle and implement. The king came to a Ugandan political machination where he was expected to administer his reign with his hands tied. He came to a kingdom that was recognized by government with no kingdom revenues, no existing financial management systems, leave alone a record of any income generating project that would generate revenue for the kingdom. This would Ultimately mean that the kingdom would be at the verge of collapse given the media reports that it would hardly manage to meet the administrative costs like water and electricity bills. Quite an embarrassment for a newly recognized kingdom, all because of partisan politics in the area. The king was supposed to be non-partisan, but as it were, without towing the ruling party line, any kingdom would suffocate or even be branded a latent enemy of the state. Indeed, this phenomenon resulted into a perfect storm that culminated into the July 2014 fatal tribal clashes; which engulfed almost the whole mountain region, which newly appointed kingdom ministers, the kingdom government, and the king himself did not expect. These fatal clashes exposed a lot of fault lines within the Rwenzururu region that should have been addressed before they escalated to a storm that would threaten the core existence and survival of the kingdom.

The July 2014 Clashes were as a result of a floated claim that a section of the Rwenzuru leadership were agitating for a so called "YIIRA" state. The kingdom had deployed a huge cabinet of over 70 individuals holding various responsibilities within the kingdom establishment, most of them semi-illiterate when it comes to governance issues, others extremely clever and rendered redundant and amidst this idleness, the king had recruited so many young people under the guise of "royal guards", a term that raised eyebrows in government circles meaning that it could be viewed as an army of the so-called Yiira state. When tribal clashed broke off, the king could not explain why there were so many royal guards even in areas where the king was not. A royal guard as the term suggests would only be necessary at the palace where the king resided. But these militia type of guards, often armed with only machetes were found in every place where there was a kingdom establishment including subcounty headquarters. The government had a duty to keep a keen eye on these guards and when the tribal clashes erupted, the government quickly stepped in to prevent what could have been a regional rebellion from occurring. It was common knowledge that the king for sure did not know about these clashes and much less having authorized them at all, but out in the media accusations were all directed at the kingdom. Many of the ministers of the kingdom were heavily involved and implicated and many were arrested, which left a cloudy atmosphere around the kingdom and frankly speaking this threatened the survival and existence of the Obusinga Bwa Rwenzururu, kingdom. The accusations directed to the kingdom were misguided since the aggressors mainly attacked government installations and not tribal communities within the region wanting to secede (pullout) from the main Rwenzururu kingdom. It therefore became a national issue that no single kingdom, let alone the Obusinga, had the ability to resolve. The king, Charles Wesley had a huge task to reconcile the warring groups, however he had another task to deal with; the uncontrollable huge cabinet. Having hired so many ministers, communication with them and holding them accountable had broken down especially since there was no pay for each portfolio appointed. There were exaggerated media reports such as what was reported in the press suggesting "Obusinga had planes full of assorted goods hovering above Kasese ready to land, to give out free goodies, and that government was hindering and stalling their landing efforts". Such miscommunications coming from disgruntled kingdom ministers sent mixed, wrong and sometimes feisty messages that showed that the kingdom was running a failed communication system. Amidst all this chaos, the king Charles came out with a very well researched brilliant rebuttal which left the government minders scratching their heads wondering where in the world Charles had gotten all the answers that would bring stability to his embattled kingdom.

BACKGROUND OF THE RWENZURURU MOVEMENT

As soon as I was elected Member of Parliament 1980 – 5 I, together with the other members of parliament from Kasese embarked on the exercise of harmonizing relations between different factions of the Rwenzururu Movement.

Prior to colonial rule, the Semliki valley was one of the most populated zones of Middle Eastern Africa. The region came to fall under the spheres of influence of the Belgians and the British. In the

Belgian region, sheer brutality, which included caning of offenders in the local communities, was applied directly; while in the British part, a system called indirect rule was used. But the indirect rule in the Rwenzori region of the British sphere of influence was put in the hands of alien community while the indigenous communities were ignored. Economic and social dynamics used by the British through the alien community, the Batoro, angered the local communities mainly the Bakonzo, leading to rebellion by the latter in 1919 – 21. The brutality by which this rebellion was quelled defined the subsequent relations between these two communities. The three leaders of the rebellion were hanged and dumped into a pit. This act was so traumatizing and humiliating to the Bakonzo people. It was the first incidence of a mass grave and also the first time a human being's remains were not buried in their history. This was done to send a clear message that any rebellious group of people would face the same type of punishment. To the Batoro the quelling of the rebellion was viewed as victory and any earlier attempt on their part to use Bakonzo traditional authority was abandoned. This marked the untold hatred between these two groups of people which would go on generation after generation until 1982. Batoro chiefs in Bakonzo areas became arrogant, brutal and discriminative. This went on under the nose of the British administrators. The Toro kingdom administration became tribalised in a multi-ethnic setting. By the 1950s, thanks to the work of religious institutions, a few Bakonzo and Bamba, the second and third largest ethnicities in Toro had gained some level of education and started questioning the status quo. Social (especially student) organizations were formed. These become the spring board for agitation that demanded for reformation of the system, coming about in the wake of the United Nations declaration and principles of human rights and self-determination. The arrogant response of the Toro administration to this agitation led to the creation of the Rwenzururu movement by the Bakonzo and Bamba in 1961 that demanded for the creation of a separate local (district) government for the two tribes. The outgoing British colonial administration relegated the decision to the post-independence government, which in its obsession to pan-Africanism resisted the sanctioning of tribal particularism at the local level. The end result was agitation for national state status by these two tribes and creating the Rwenzururu United Kingdom in 1962. The agitation for the kingdom was thus addressed to the United Nations organization. The then Rwenzururu delegation to the United Nations were arrested in Rwanda as they were trying to travel to Adis Ababa, to attend a UN meeting and present their demands.

Chapter 22

CONFLICT IN THE RWENZURURU UNITED KINGDOM

The refusal by Toro government to effect reforms as demanded by the Bamba and Bakonzo and the denial by the Ugandan government to grant a separate district to the Baamba and Bakonzo communities led to the militarization of the agitation and the formation of a kingdom whose king withdrew into the thick Rwenzori mountain forests. These acts led to divided opinion among the leaders of the movement so that while one group opted for open fighting, the other believed in continued agitation through negotiation.

The central government attempted to exploit this division by supporting those who believed in a negotiated road map against the militants. The result was that the militants, from their forest sanctuary started killing leaders of the other group whom they saw as traitors to the cause. This situation continued up to the time when the immediate post-independence government was toppled in a military coup on January 25, 1971.

The military administration of Idi Amin tried to settle the situation by granting separate districts to both the Bamba and Bakonzo in 1974. However, this arrangement was not acceptable to the militants who intensified their activities especially when they had acquired some guns, ammunitions and firearms training from

Congolese rebels. This is the stage at which, after the elections of 1980 by which I was elected an MP, we the elected politicians took center stage and initiated negotiations with the militants to abandon militarism, create peace and participate in what we saw as the beginning of development in the area for the first time in the history of Uganda. The outburst of Education was the cause for celebration.

Our efforts bore fruit. In 1982, the Rwenzururu king, Charles Wesley Mumbere Iremangoma, in what he called change of methods of fighting, handed in his mountain government to the elected government of Uganda. He did this in return for government letting him remain as chief elder of his people (at the age of 30), offer of a study scholarship abroad for himself, absorption of the administrators of the kingdom into the administration of the districts and some of the ex-fighters [in present terms called "royal guards"] into the Uganda national army. These negotiations and agreements took place at the Nsenyi catholic parish headquarters in the presence of Ugandan army chief of staff Major General David Oyit Ojok (RIP) and Charles Wesley Mumbere Iremangoma himself. As members of parliament, we were witnesses to this accord that was to bring ultimate peace in the region.

This negotiated arrangement led to three years of peace in the area for the first time since 1962 and also meaningful development since Lugard's creation of Toro kingdom in 1893.

THE CURRENT IMPASSE IN THE RWENZORI REGION

This period of bliss was short-lived. Immediately after the 1980 general elections, one Yoweri Museveni [now a general] after getting defeated in his bid for the presidency of the republic of Uganda, declared war against the elected government. His party, the Uganda Patriotic Movement UPM, received one seat in parliament, by one Chripus Kiyonga of Kasese district. The election was viewed according to him as rigged, just because he did not win a seat that was hotly contested by the Democratic party. He lost to a Democratic party candidate, Mr. Sam Kutesa, his own brother-in-law. In February 1981, Museveni started a war that saw him ascend the presidency of the Republic of Uganda in January 1986.

Because Buganda had a natural hatred for Obote and his Uganda Peoples Congress (UPC) which had won the elections, Mr. Museveni took advantage of this hatred and staged his rebellion in the central region - the Buganda region. He received massive support especially in this region and wrecked untold havoc that demonized and disoriented the elected UPC government. He and his supporters mounted massive campaigns abroad to discredit the government and convince the West [colonial Masters] that elections were not free and fair. The West [colonial masters] tried to convince Dr. Obote to negotiate peace with Mr. Museveni, but Obote would not accept. He contended that he could not negotiate with a fellow who lost elections and was shooting at buses and ambulances to justify his cause. While refusing to negotiate with what he called bandits, Obote was having issues within his own army that had been disoriented by the fighting rebels. There were tribal divisions between the Acholi who were majority and the bantus who were minority as well as being considered sympathizers of the bandits. After losing his trusted chief of staff Maj. Gen. David Oyite Ojok, Obote could not sustain a united force against the bandits even when they were on the brink of defeat. Mr. Museveni had fled the bush to live in Sweden, while his diminished gang of rebels fled in retreat to the west of the country to hide in the Mountains of the Moon in Bunyangabo county. The whole country was affected by this rebel fighting. As they fled from Luwero to the west, there were several roadblocks mounted by the army which mistreated civilians to the point of increasing hatred for the army. Almost on the brink of defeating Museveni rebels, this disorientation of government and the fatigue resulting from the 4 years of bush war led to a military coup by two Generals. These generals notoriously referred to as the Okellos, thus Bazilio Olara Okello and Tito Okello (not related), were from the Acholi tribe, that had the bulk of soldiers in the army. After declaring themselves in power and knowing that Obote had fled the country, Bazilio Olara Okello went on Radio Uganda to call upon Yoweri Museveni, whom they had been fighting for 4 years, to come to a negotiation table. Once the Okellos made the call to the rebels to come for talks, the Okello soldiers stopped pursuing the bandits, while waited for Museveni to respond. Meanwhile, the retreating bandits took advantage of the call and started massive recruitment starting with the disgruntled bantu soldiers within the Okello army. They got overwhelming support from an exhausted population. The harassments at roadblocks and the looting of civilians' monies and property had become the trademark of the Okello soldiers. Anybody who came up with a formula to stop this would be very quickly welcome. Museveni had that formula, having acquired the best talent to mobilize fighting rebels from his experience in Mozambique and Tanzania in preparation for fighting Amin. He mobilized and got support from the other fighting groups and defeated the military government within six months forming a government of National Unity made up of persons from the entire political spectrum in the country. What Museveni did not do was to include the Rwenzururu players in this arrangement. A government of National Unity without Rwenzururu players would leave the Kasese region in a dissatisfied mode which would easily exacerbate violence, something they had been good at for many years.

This act ended the peace that had culminated from the negotiated arrangement of king Charles Wesley Mumbere Iremangoma who was viewed as a collaborator of the overthrown elected government. The settlements the previous regime had reached with Rwenzururu veterans, through the members of parliament were not honored, the scholarship for the king was cancelled, and some of the institutions established during the 4 years of our regional stability and development were halted. The new regime systematically worked to dismantle our achievements. Since 1986 the Rwenzori region has become an arena of war.

In the first place, the chiefs (former administrators in Mumbere's bush government) who had been absorbed in local government were dismissed without preamble. Then followed the cancellation of

Mumbere's study scholarship in the USA where he had been for 2 year (by 1986) and confiscation of properties offered for his resettlement. Plans to resettle the ex-fighters of the Rwenzururu kingdom were abandoned and civil servants were purged. Political leaders who had participated in the negotiated peace were thrown into prisons and quite a number fled into exile while others were murdered (a colleague MP from the area, Hon Lt Tom Baluku being a case in point.)

In other regions of the country, especially in northern and eastern Uganda a similar situation prevailed leading to alleged and real rebel groupings that became excuse of mass killings of innocent Ugandans. Innocent people who were suspected of supporting rebel groups were branded as lodgers in the "panda gari" operations and dumped in Luzira, where majority perished without ever seeing a Judge.

But the new regime quickly adopted populist methods of work sounding as champions of women emancipation and the disabled, declaring free pre university education (UPE, USE) abolishing graduated tax and brainwashing citizens by creating cadres recruitment centres. One of the most important populist activities of the regime was the rewriting of the national constitution. Its effect on the Rwenzori region is probably the single cause of the current political impasse therein. Article 246 of the constitution allowed for restoration of kingdoms in the country that had been abolished in 1966 and also provided for the creation of any such cultural institutions by any community that so wished.

The old kingdoms of Buganda, Bunyoro and Busoga were restored and in my view Toro kingdom was once again recreated as was done by Frederick Lugard in 1893. But whereas Lugard recreated the kingdom by adding to it the mountainous regions of Rwenzori (to include the counties of Busongora, Bunyangabo, Bwamba and parts of Burahya) the new kingdom was reconstituted without Bukonjo, Bwamba and Busongora. The constitution had not quantified those who should "so wish" thereby giving the regime leeway to reward or punish any community in accordance with its populist and patronage tendencies. So that Ankole kingdom with millions of people "so wishing" has been rejected while some communities with less than a hundred thousand people have been granted cultural institution status. The Basongora in the Rwenzori region are close to 25,000 people and are boasting of a cultural institution. But the Banyankole who are millions have not been powerful enough to deserve recognition as a cultural institution. I wonder what happened to Ankole kingdom where Museveni hails from!

In 1982 the central government neither abolished the Rwenzururu kingdom nor recognised it. But Charles Wesley Mumbere was referred to as chief elder with a multi-ethnic cultural council of elders. This arrangement had not been accorded to any other former kingdom and endured until 1998. Following the promulgation of the constitution of the republic of Uganda in 1995 Charles Wesley Mumbere who was still stranded in the USA taking up jobs as health care aide after the cancellation of his study scholarship, started demanding for recognition of Rwenzururu kingdom. It should be noted here that Wesley, having led the movement after the death of his father Isaya Mukirania, has the capacity to mobilize his subjects and form a resistance that would stick to their demands. The 1995 constitution rekindled the demand for recognition, which immediately reawakened division in the "kingdom". The situation was that the local political leaders in the region, probably viewing the kingship as an alternative power centre became vehemently opposed to the idea. This was in contradiction to the wishes of the majority of the people. The resultant conflict was so tense that government found it necessary to task one Makerere University researcher Kabann Kabananukye to investigate the issues and make recommendations. The investigations revealed that the demand was popular with 85% of the people in support 12% opposed and 3 % undecided. These statistics were strongly rejected by those opposed to the scheme of recognition.

All manner of maneuver was applied until 1998 when Charles Wesley Mumbere was accused of involvement with a new rebel group operating from the Democratic Rrepublic of Congo (DRC) that had attacked Kasese, Kabarole, Bundibugyo in 1996 - the Allied

Democratic Forces (ADF). This allegation almost culminated into violence, forcing government to charge the vice chairman of the ruling National Resistance Movement, Al Haji Moses Kigongo to establish the facts. A conference of elders and stakeholders at Mweya Safari lodge ended in a stalement leading government to call Charles to return to Uganda to defend himself. After he had been cleared, Charles intensified his demand for recognition and in 2005 government appointed a ministerial committee to investigate the controversy surrounding the struggle for recognition of the Rwenzururu kingdom. The committee recommended *inter alia*, that the kingdom be recognised. This is the only cultural institution that has had two commissions of inquiries appointed to ascertain its recognition.

On October 19, 2009 the kingdom was recognized ending 47years of a bitter struggle. In 1982, the then government ended what was considered the 20yrs of bitterness and the NRM government skillfully ended the ultimate struggle crediting President Museveni but leaving many wondering why he waited for such a long time.

But apparently the conflict escalated albeit having caused some tranquility from 2009 to 2011. In those three years, the king had gained massive popularity, with massive rallies at coronation ceremonies, something that raised eye brows of the government. The recognition would become a new headache for the political leaders of the time.

Chapter 23

FRESH ISSUES OF CONFLICT

Starting with the year 2012 misunderstandings started between government and the newly recognised Rwenzururu kingdom. That year the Omusinga Charles Wesley Mumbere, Iremangoma was barred from making a routine visit to his subjects in the Bundibugyo part of his kingdom. He was refused to visit his subjects at the lake side village of Kasenyi in Kasese district. Soon after, the Baamba were granted a cultural institution status and soon after other small communities within the kingdom declared themselves to be cultural institutions as provided for in the constitution. All this was being done without explanations to Rwenzururu kingdom. This caused disaffections of the kingdom towards government as all efforts to understand what was going on was denied. The government approach became the catalyst for massive divisions in the region.

In July 2014 unarmed youths attacked security establishments in Bundibugyo, Ntoroko and Kasese districts. This act was tribalised and the Baamba in Bundibugyo massacred Bakonzo youths who had attacked military barracks nearby, killing nearly 100 of them. Government arrested many people including some kingdom ministers. But between October 2015 and April 2016 relations normalized between the kingdom and the government

After April 2016 and the general elections of February where all the NRM candidates lost all the top elective positions in the district, unexplained events started taking place. In November the king was arrested, his palace was burnt with heavy artillery fire and over one hundred people killed including babies and women. About 200 others were arrested and still remain in prison, three years down the road. The arrogance of local ruling party leaders bamboozled the population in the district which was already traumatized by the events leading to the massacre at the palace and so far government has not made any sense of the situation. There are many people still in detention while government is facing charges in the international criminal court.

I believe here that the peoples' attitude to the NRM has been shaped by local NRM leadership's arrogance and divisive methods of work. Even the party supporters in the district are categorized into cream and dilute in accordance with the whims of the party leaders. Attempts to educate the masses about NRM are limited to party members without any effort to recruit new members. And this sets a dangerous precedent regarding attitudes towards development. The government has not clearly formulated any policy or procedure about dealing with a situation that has lasted decades. It looks like no one in the region is willing to learn from history and to do the right thing for the benefit of future generations to follow.

GENERAL OBSERVATIONS

The problems in the Rwenzori region go back in history and mainly hinge on power sharing. Around 1830, a runaway prince of Bunyoro kingdom rebelled against his father, king of Bunyoro and declared himself king in one of the counties in his father's realm. He succeeded. However, rivalry among his sons for succession weakened the young kingdom until Kabalega, king of Bunyoro from about 1870 reintegrated Toro into Bunyoro. One of the princes, Kasagama fled his kingdom. In the 1890s captain Fredrick Lugard of the British East Africa Company in a bid to contain Kabalega of Bunyoro reinstated Kasagama and by the 1900 Toro agreement he created a larger Toro kingdom than Kaboyo had established earlier. He annexed the mountain regions including the whole of Busongora, Bunyangabo, Burahya and Bwamba. Hereto these areas were normally parts of Bunyoro kingdom. British colonial polices established in Toro the scourge of tribalism that was to lead to rebellion in 1917 – 21 and again in 1962. This was not peculiar to Toro but here it had the effect of bolstering one tribe, the Batoro against the others.

In 1967 the government of independent Uganda abolished kingdoms including Lugard's Toro. But the NRM regime created its own Toro when it restored the kingdoms of Buganda, Bunyoro and Busoga. By this time the Amin regime had farther demolished Lugard's Toro. Current Toro is thus a new political battle ground. Each of these Toros had its own attendant challenges that in part explain violence in the region.

Under these circumstances, social-economic transformation in the region has been concentrated in the accessible plain lands, leaving the highlands out. Yet these highlands are heavily inhabited. The population up there feels left out and not part of Uganda.

At the same time the rugged mountain terrain and the impenetrable forest thereon provide a safe haven for any renegade against the law in Uganda. The Rwenzururu movement and nascent Rwenzururu kingdom survived in this environment for twenty years in spite of sporadic government military deployment to dislodge it. This is coupled with the fact that the Congo – Uganda border is highly porous because the borderland people are the same culturally. On the Congo side, this is exacerbated by the ineffectiveness or near absence of the Congolese government administration in the region. This in part explains the appearing genocidal murders of Congolese citizens there and general assumption that the perpetrators could be Ugandan military soldiers in pursuit of anti-government groups like the ADF. In the southern part of the Congolese eastern province of north Kivu, the Rwandese forces are also having a field day claiming to be pursuing the escapee perpetrators of the 1994 genocide in Rwanda called "Interahamwe".

Furthermore, and especially in the case of Kasese the government neglected all the achievements of the negotiated settlement of the previous regime to end the 20-year freedom struggle. In the first place the Rwenzururu ex-fighters had not been settled and no effort has been made to revive the effort to resettle them. Since 1986 when the National Resistance Movement (NRM) took the reins of governance, these ex-fighters have seen revival of the discrimination meted to them during the Frederick Lugard regime in Toro kingdom. As explained earlier in this book, education was not extended to them. From 1981 to 1986 many schools were set up to close this gap. Consequently, very many youths have accessed education. But there is no employment for them. Even when this is a national (indeed a global) phenomenon, the educated youth together with the elderly ex-fighters look at it differently. And, despite the 1995 national constitution declaring that communities could set up cultural institutions, it took long for government to recognize the Rwenzururu kingdom as a cultural institution. Yet within two years of the eventual recognition of this kingdom in 2009 several other such institutions raised their heads and received government nod. This led to even limiting the movement of the king to tour his kingdom and guide his people towards social (cultural) and economic development. Confrontations between the youth and government security agencies became rampant climaxing in the youth attacks against government security personnel. Response to this was seen as being unreasonably intense. Over one hundred Bakonzo tribesmen were killed in Bwamba and buried in mass graves.

In the aftermath of 2016 elections where the ruling party suffered heavy defeat, security deployment in the region was stepped up and trumped up allegations were made that the kingdom was planning a secessionist mission to form a state, "the yiira state". Innocent youths probably unemployed, idle and disorderly alleged to be pursuing this this were gunned down in broad day light forcing many of them to flee to the king palace. Any government established by law seeing their sovereignty challenged by the so-called Yiira secessionists would do the same to protect their borders. Their presence there was dubbed rebel recruitment and the king was alleged to be in compliance. On

November 27, 2016 the king was arrested and after removing him from the palace, the place was shelled by artillery fire and over one hundred people were killed including woman and young children; most of who had gone to the palace either to deliver food or to search for food. Nearly two hundred other people were arrested and still languish in prison without trial three years down the road.

For a long, time successive governments in post-independence Uganda have attempted to tackle some of these issues. But they have each lacked the will to complete their missions despite well-articulated action guidelines. The National Resistance Movement has had the longest time with this violence. It has the capacity and resources to end this violence only if it can expend the will to do it. They need to consult more, listen more and negotiate more. The release of money to facilitate certain sections of society will not solve the conflict. The handing out of envelopes stuffed with shillings will not either

Chapter 24

INTERNAL CONFLICT AND CHAOTIC EXECUTIVE LEADERSHIP

On August 15, 1982, the "omusinga" Charles Wesley Mumbere had stressed in his coming down speech that coming down was not a surrender, but a change of method. This statement had a two faced meaning, first it implied the coming down was an abandonment of violence and using pen and paper to pursue peace and dignity for the people. Secondly it implied that while the original kingdom establishment had been sustained crudely by a privy council with four "prime ministers" during the 20 years of bitterness, thus Fenehasi Kisokeranio, Mr. Bawalana, Mr. Mulima and the last "mulerembere" Mr. Yeremiya Kihugho who at the negotiated peace settlement became the district administrative officer; the new method would emulate the central government leadership with executive powers invested in the Obusinga prime minister position. The omusinga had a parade of very qualified individuals who thought an opportunity for employment had struck close to home.

In his search for peace and reconciliation, the king sought to include all sectors of the community to participate in every social fabric of the kingdom so that the leadership is seen to be balanced. The constitution had already taken cognizance of the diversity of cultures in the region. Representatives from the region to the Constituent

Assembly had ensured that the various communities were included. This has now been exploited especially by those elements in the country who believe in small groups that can easily be patronized and used to enhance dismantling the bases of the 1982 reconciliation accord negotiated by the Obote leadership.

ENOCH MUHINDO - Acting Prime Minister, Rwenzururu

The Obusinga Bwa Rwenzururu at recognition had no short or long term plans for development. Opportunity had not been provided to allow for building and consolidation of systems of operation. Moving from a Privy Council form of leadership to modern form of civilized governance posed huge challenges. The king was forced to create a glaringly and meaninglessly large cabinet without programs to implement. The chief executive of this body, dubbed

"Omulerembera" or Prime Minister has inexplicably been changed annually. In the ten years of its existence, the institution has had nine (9) persons in that capacity with the current vague arrangement (Prime Ministerial Commission) being in office for the longest period. There have been only three substantively appointed prime ministers who included; Mr. Constantine Bwambale (2009 – 2010), Hon. Loice Bwambale (2010 - 2011) came in an acting position after Mr. Constantine Bwambale had resigned on account that the kingdom business was taking a huge toll on the running of his own personal business. She was notoriously removed on account that as a woman she would not perform the cultural rituals that embroidered the institution. On her exit, Henry Kandabu (2011 – 2012), Syauswa Ivan (2011), Jehoiada Mutooro (2011) all with no experience or no history with the Rwenzururu movement and could not last beyond a year. Almost on the verge of collapse, the king called on the Speaker, **Enoch Muhindo** (2014 -2015) to fill the vacuum and bring the institution back to life. In an acting position while doubling as speaker, he brought in some stability before handing it to Noah Nzaghale (interruptedly 2014 - 2016). In addition, Jeremiah Mutooro (2016) held office in acting capacity. One Thembo Kitsumbire took advantage of his acting capacity to usurp the powers of Jeremiah Mutooro in 2016 – 7 in what I will call silent palace coup citing the fact that the latter was not permanently residing at the Obusinga headquarters. Kitsumbire concentrated on consolidating his usurped position at whatever cost leading to the disaster of November 2016.

The problem has all along been that the cultural institution has no financial base and yet some of these people looked at the office as an employment opportunity. Relations between the institution and Government deteriorated especially in 2012 – 2014 and again in 2016 with the confusion as to who held the office. By the time the Omusinga put his foot down in late 2016 the damage was apparently already done, and misunderstandings between the state and the institution all concentrated in that year culminated in the dark days of November 2016. The institution was once again at the mercy of the central authority. Nearly three years of the prime ministerial commission have achieved some internal tranquility but relations with government remain uncertain, as the Omusinga remains a prisoner together with about two hundred of his subjects. Attempts to disentangle this situation seem to be hampered by political opportunists who have petitioned the International Criminal Court(ICC) to scrutinize the 2016 massacre at and burning of the Omusinga palace.

The contradictions have further been complicated by disgruntled ex Rwenzururu fighters who have been generally ignored in the institution they struggled for. They were hardly made to participate in the administration of the recognized institution. Their twenty years of struggle deemed to have been unrewarded and their role in influencing the high turnover in the implementation organs of the institution cannot be ignored.

The institution remains very popular. The Omusinga is extremely popular. But for the Omusinga the biblical saying that a prophet is not without honor except in his own town is apparently applicable. Charles Wesley Mumbere's family is a contradiction, as it does not provide the necessary model of harmony in the community. There is little lost between him and his siblings. One of the siblings who had been politically active crossed from the FDC party into the ruling NRM party on condition that if he swore by the NRM manifesto and kept his oath, he would be rewarded with a ministerial position. The NRM leadership delivered on their promise appointed him a minister of state, causing a rift between the royal siblings. This ultimate betray led to total confusion in the palace when the queen mother died and her burial saga culminated in a loss of relationship with the embattled king who remained under house arrest.

Chapter 25

A QUEEN MOTHER DIES, AND CHAOS ERUPTS

In every African tradition and especially the Bakonzo, a death of a loved one brings family together however; emotional impact can also tear survivors apart. This happened to be the case for the Rwenzururu royal family. The death of the Queen mother, Christine Bira Mukirania on June 11, 2019 threw the entire "royal family" and the bakonzo tribe in disarray. Why did this have to be that way? The kingdom does not have to date a burial place for "royals" as well they do not have an established place, which would be called theirs. The original king, Isaya Mukirane was buried in the mountains, an area that have attracted suggestions from certain schools of thought to be a Centre for attraction in form of either a museum or a tourist site. This, if well thought through would bring in revenue for the Obusinga. A kingdom Shrine, a monument, or a tribal symbol could be erected to attract historians and tourists to visit. Plans to effect these schools of thought have stalled due to financial capacity as well as intellectual capacity to put the mechanism in place. But also, the bankruptcy of ideas and initiatives that the regime has manifested over the population. The population has been rendered useless mentally, spiritually and economically. There is so much idleness and clamor for the survival of the fittest. Dictator Hitler once explained that his success to supremacy was due to the German people not understanding the issues around them. "*Our political problems appeared complicated. The German people could make nothing of them... I...reduced them to the simplest terms. The masses realized this and followed me.*" This statement is good for Ugandans, and the Bakonzo are not exempted. The people of Uganda and the Bankonzo in particular did not understand the political, cultural, and economic implications of the NRM government; therefore, they had no choice but to follow. The death of the queen mother brought in confusion, which found fertile soil for chaos. Over the years the government has been in power, 34 years in counting, the systems had been quite engaged, if I may use Mussolini's quote about "plucking a chicken feather by feather" so that people will not notice the loss of their freedoms until it is too late. Ugandans have been reduced to that quote, they have lost their freedoms indirectly, they have lost their resources through the credit unions, they have lost their national treasures that have been sold to multi-millionaires so that the gap between the rich and the poor widens. The bakonzo have been victims too that even the queen mother who had no blood or cultural relations to the president, had been adopted as "sister" in order to be facilitated for survival. She like other many nationals had been a beneficiary of the "envelop" scheme that the head of state carries and distributes to those he deems deserving. Once a chicken loses all its feathers, it is reduced to just being a follower of the only one who will provide. They cannot fend for themselves; they become dependent just like beggars. The bakonzo besides the elite class have been reduced to beggars and the royal family was not exempt. The queen mother was enjoying free movement with a government-donated vehicle, free gas. One of the sons who had the title of "chief prince" was once a member of the opposition, a very powerful district power broker as a pillar of the opposition. Once all the feathers were plucked off, he was reduced to almost a common subject. Being smart, the chief Prince denounced his party affiliations in the FDC (forum for Democratic Change) which had nothing to offer, and crossed over the ruling NRM (National Resistance Movement) party. At his crossing, he was subjected to a sworn oath to uphold the principles of the ruling party and perhaps to endeavor to turn the district, which had notoriously become opposition, die hard, to the ruling party. Of course, every crossing to any party has some give and take benefits. It is believed he was promised a suitable "potato" befitting a crossover, which he would use to re assert his influence in the district as well as in the Obusinga royals. This happened while his brother was incarcerated in prison as a suspected accomplice over the murders that occurred at the palace as it was being destroyed. This family betrayal did not sit well with the Obusinga subjects (ordinary people) who saw their institution almost losing meaning in front of their very eyes. The queen mother died on June 11 at Kilembe hospital and later that day taken to Fort Portal Hospital for body treatment. While the body was in Fort Portal, the chief prince who had been rewarded with a much thicker and delicious potato from the NRM regime used his influence to take the body for burial out to Kirindi, their ancestral origin. This was against the wish of the queen mother who, it is believed had wished to be buried on a piece of land she purchased with the money his "adopted" brother gave her while she was still alive. This piece of land was not yet developed. At Nyamirangara the chief prince had constructed his village home, and it was hoped that the queen mother would be buried here. Plans changed for strategic political reason as the chief prince had won a political seat in the district of Bundibugyo where he needed to consolidate his influence as he asserted in his speech at the burial that "he had returned home" by bringing "his" mother home for burial.

The rest of the family boycotted going to Kirindi as it was against their mother's wish. One of the sons, William even threatened to drug his brother to courts of law for defying family protocols. The ultimate betrayal came about when the chief prince was asked why he defied protocol, and he replied arrogantly that his brothers were hooligans, (erighalha) as quoted on radio Messiah, a local broadcasting station on the eve of celebration of life. The chief prince did mention that they are three boys left behind by their mother, and each of them, if they have homes should go and celebrate the life of their mother individually. He implied that king Charles did not have a home, and challenged him to come and organize his own celebration of life while offering to attend if invited. This culminated into appeals from community and church leaders to urge the family to not wash their dirty linen in public. The mayor of Kasese Godfrey Kabyanga called upon the chief prince to deal with their family issues in their mothers living room instead of the streets, which was painting a bad image of the institution they represented. The reverend Ezira Mukonzo called for peace as he preached like the summon on the mount. "that blessed are the peace makers for they will be called God's people". The reverend offered to be a mediator between William and Christopher who were at serious log heads before they could meet with their older brother, the "king" Charles Wesley Mumbere. The king, who was under house arrest, was by court order prohibited from traveling outside of Kampala, Wakiso and Jinja. That meant that he could not travel to Kasese, but through his lawyers, he had secured a court order that allowed him to go and mourn his mother. However, as the confusion in the family intensified, he strategically chose not to travel to the Rwenzururu region. The queen mother was then laid to rest amid chaos between family members majority of whom boycotted going to Kirindi for burial while one son saw it as a political victory to bring "his" mother home, as he termed it.

Chapter 26

THE JOURNEY TO REDEMPTION

For survival, the Rwenzururu kingdom will have to first appreciate that it was recognized by the state of the republic of Uganda and therefore adhere to the statutory provisions of the state. It must also internally appreciate and harmonize the roles of all the stakeholders – chiefdoms, clans, the diverse ethnic composition and the ex-fighters. There is need for institution stop running like a political government and revert to cultural leadership with fewer ministerial positions. or better still to not all them ministerial positions. Perhaps giving them a title which is culturally appropriate since most of these positions might be managed on volunteer basis.

The politicians of the sub region should not be given an opening, which will allow them to manipulate the institution for political gains. The popularity of the institution among the Bayira and Bamba makes it vulnerable and open to interpretation when it comes to political parties.

While "his majesty" Omusinga Wesley remains under house arrest pending trial, or case dismissal, new development of unexpected important visitor arose where His wife, the Lady queen Agnes emerged after a long time of silence and absence with a message of peace and reconciliation, something that left many people perplexed. She arrived unexpectedly in an army chopper financed by the government and landed at the Kasese airfield. On arrival on Kasese soil after almost three years, while attending to her husband, she delivered a speech sent by Omusinga Charles. She spoke passionately about the redemption of an institution that was on the verge of collapse and castigated politicians and schemers who masquerade in the name of Obusinga to agitate for "Yiira" state. She categorically denounced them as schemers who do not promote peace. She said, the king does not support the creation of a "state". The Obusinga bwa Rwenzururu was about a cultural kingdom for the welfare of the citizens of Uganda living in the Rwenzori sub-region. At another rally, she told her listeners that the king disassociated himself and the Obusinga institution from the ICC (International Criminal Court) case that hangs over Uganda government for the massacre of over 100 people at the palace, which was burnt by the state army. As she goes around the sub-region preaching peace and reconciliation, and as the king's messenger without political interference, questions remain; will this be the redemption of a people who appear confused, deeply frustrated, and knowing their popular king remains in custody; or will his release coincide with the launching of political campaigns as elections draws near? The mystry of the Rwenzururu will forever continue to allude the status quo. What the people of the sub-region need are services that promote the wellbeing of everyone such as services that fight against ignorance, poverty and disease. The message to fight against those evils ought to be coming from the government that would like to appear to side with the people.

Epilogue

THE UNFORGETTABLE MYTH BECAME REAL

On October 19, 2009 Charles Wisley Irema Ngoma was celebrating what was called the 43rd Coronation Anniversary. The president of Uganda Yoweri Museveni was present and one of the most important announcements he made was to recognize the existence of the Rwenzururu Kingdom, which had been the subject of a bitter struggle for many years. At a colorful ceremony at the Kilembe Mines Golf Club, more than 30,000 people came to witness the recognition of the Obusinga. Delegations of high ranking officials came from the Democratic Republic of Congo where the Bayira number to almost 5 million as opposed to about 1 million in Uganda. The myth that kept the people together as they collectively fought for what was inherently theirs came to real life. In recent years there had been oppositions to the recognition of this institution. Various insignificant kings have masqueraded as rightful kings. Politicians of various political parties had hoped that these mushrooming would be kings would pull support from the indigenous people in Kasese and Bundibugyo, but the rightful King who had lived in the United States for over 25 years prevailed. A new Rwenzururu anthem was played on that day. It is on record as the best melodious anthem of modern times. The anthem tells the story of what Rwenzururu kingdom is all about.

Omusinga/King Charles Wesley Mumbere with Queen Agnes Mumbere on the morning of the 43rd anniversary of Rwenzururu Kingdom. On this day October 19, President Yoweri Museveni and Dr. Chrispus Kiyonga, addressed Mumbere as 'His Majesty Omusinga Irema-Ngoma' for the first time. GLORY IS TO THE ALMIGHTY GOD THAT WE CAN SEE THIS IN REAL LIFE TIME.

THE REAL BUHIKIRA ROYAL PALACE – KASESE TOWN

CPSIA information can be obtained
at www.ICGtesting.com
Printed in the USA
LVHW090802260220
648218LV00001B/2